THE ROAD TO EQUALITY

AMERICAN WOMEN
SINCE 1962

THE YOUNG OXFORD HISTORY OF WOMEN IN THE UNITED STATES

Nancy F. Cott, *General Editor*

THE ROAD TO EQUALITY

AMERICAN WOMEN SINCE 1962

William H. Chafe

OXFORD UNIVERSITY PRESS

New York • Oxford

For My Mother

Oxford University Press

Oxford   New York   Toronto
Delhi Bombay Calcutta Madras Karachi
Kuala Lumpur Singapore Hong Kong Tokyo
Nairobi Dar es Salaam Cape Town
Melbourne Auckland Madrid
and associated companies in
Berlin   Ibadan

Library of Congress Cataloging-in-Publication Data

Chafe, William Henry.
The road to equality : American women since 1962 / William Chafe.
p. cm. — (The Young Oxford history of women in the United States ; v. 10)
Includes bibliographical references and index.
ISBN 0-19-508325-3
ISBN 0-19-508830-1 (series)
1. Women—United States—Juvenile literature. 2. Feminism—United States—Juvenile literature.
3. Equality—United States—Juvenile literature. 4. United States—Social conditions—1960-1980.
5. United States—Social conditions—1980- [1. Feminism. 2. Women's rights 3. United States—Social conditions.]
I. Title II. Series
HQ1421.C43   1994
305.42'0973—dc20
93-39769
CIP
AC

1 3 5 7 9 8 6 4 2
Printed in the United States of America
on acid-free paper

Design: Leonard Levitsky
Picture Research: Lisa Kirchner, Laura Kreiss

Cover: Celebrating Women's Lives by Miriam Schapiro, 1986.
Frontispiece: A poster issued in the 1970s by the National Organization for Women (NOW).

CONTENTS

INTRODUCTION

It might be said with only small exaggeration that the situation of women has altered more in the past 30 years than it had in the preceding 300 years. The 1960s, 1970s, and 1980s were decades of vast changes in the world at large—in patterns of technology and industry, in the emergence of new nations, in global and environmental awareness. But perhaps no change is more obvious than the recognition of women as economic providers and the emergence of women into roles of prominence and public authority formerly held by men only. Though this is a worldwide development, it is especially vital in the United States.

As this book shows, the woman's movement that started in the 1960s transformed ways of thinking about men's and women's destinies. Stimulated by the decade's campaigns for civil rights for African Americans, attacks on the "establishment," antiwar activism, and attempts to create a "counterculture," American women organized to confront prejudices about and stereotypes of feminine character and capabilities, to claim rights as individuals, and to upset the hierarchy of power between the sexes that made it a "man's world." Their activism, intersecting with economic and demographic trends, created a new era. In the current era, attitudes and practices in areas as diverse as work, sexuality, emotion, and politics have vastly changed

The T-shirt worn by the woman (bottom right) at a Washington, D.C., rally in 1976 reflects the extent to which many men felt threatened by women's increased presence in the work force, particularly in professional positions.

to accommodate women's presence and demands—yet women themselves are not united in what their presence and demands amount to. Feminists who divide on many issues would agree that the balance of power between women and men has not clearly broken up or shifted; continuities in the division of labor by sex as well as in norms of masculinity and femininity show remarkable persistence. As this book, which discusses the years since 1960, eloquently reveals, the consequences of change are often turmoil and uncertainty—backlash as well as gains.

This book is part of a series that covers the history of women in the United States from the 17th through the 20th century. Traditional historical writing has dealt almost entirely with men's lives because men have, until very recently, been the heads of state, the political officials, judges, ministers, and business leaders who wielded the most visible and recorded power. But for several recent decades, new interest has arisen in social and cultural history, where common people are the actors who create trends and mark change as well as continuity. An outpouring of research and writing on women's history has been part of this trend to look at individuals and groups who have not held the reins of rule in their own hands but nonetheless participated in making history. The motive to address and correct sexual inequality in society has also vitally influenced women's history, on the thinking that knowledge of the past is essential to creating justice for the future.

The histories in this series look at many aspects of women's lives.

Clad in academic gowns, women marched in front of the U.S. Supreme Court in an attempt to influence its decisions in such cases as Roe v. Wade. *Their banner bears the ironic message, "If men got pregnant, abortion would be sacred."*

The books ask new questions about the course of American history. How did the type and size of families change, and what difference did that make in people's lives? What expectations for women differed from those for men, and how did such expectations change over the centuries? What roles did women play in the economy? What form did women's political participation take when they could not vote? And how did politics change when women did gain full citizenship? How did women work with other women who were like or unlike them, as well as with men, for social and political goals? What sex-specific constraints or opportunities did they face? The series aims to understand the diverse women who have peopled American history by investigating their work and leisure, family patterns, political activities, forms of organization, and outstanding accomplishments. Standard events of American history, from the settling of the continent to the American Revolution, the Civil War, industrialization, American entry onto the world stage, and world wars, are all here, too, but seen from the point of view of women's experiences. Together, the answers to new questions and the treatment of old ones from women's points of view make up a compelling narrative of four centuries of history in the United States.

—Nancy F. Cott

THE
YOUNG OXFORD
HISTORY OF WOMEN
IN THE
UNITED STATES

CHAPTER 1

LET US BEGIN

The signs were auspicious for change. "The torch has been passed to a new generation of Americans," a young President said. After years of being governed by those born in the 19th century, the generation that came of age during the World War II era had finally surged to power, bringing with it a new tone of urgency and activism. "Ask not what your country can do for you," the President said, "but what you can do for your country." As if to symbolize the changing of the guard, new attention began to be paid to problems and issues that for too long had been hidden in the shadows. It was as though the sun had risen in a new way, suddenly illuminating areas that were crying out for systematic action.

Although John F. Kennedy was not known then—or since—as a feminist, one of his first acts was to create a Presidential Commission on the Status of Women, naming Eleanor Roosevelt, the most venerated and admired woman in the country, as its honorary chair. In some ways this initiative was inadvertent, unconnected to Kennedy's far more conventional concerns with foreign policy and economic growth. Nevertheless, the commission was an unintentional reflection of the air of incipient unrest that was making its way through society as people awakened to new challenges. Students on the nation's

The inauguration of President John F. Kennedy in 1961 ushered in a new era of hope for the younger generation. He said in his inaugural address, "The torch has been passed to a new generation of Americans, born in this century, tempered by a hard and bitter war" and committed to doing whatever was necessary to "defend freedom at its hour of maximum peril."

campuses started to discuss political reform and social injustice. Young blacks in the American South boldly announced that henceforth black people would not accept being seated only in the balconies at movie theaters, using rest rooms marked "Colored Only," or standing up at lunch counters rather than sitting down with other customers. The nation had even started to read again about poverty in America and how more than 20 percent of American citizens—primarily old people and children, women, and blacks—were living below the "poverty level." And this was all happening within a framework of excited optimism. Something *should* be done. Something *would* be done.

If a group of journalists had gathered around a table in 1962, they would not have been likely to select changes in women's lives as one of the major stories to emerge from these years. After all, politics as defined by John Kennedy was still a "macho" game, with the Cold War dominant, events such as the Cuban Missile Crisis the real testing points, and even civil rights more a showdown between male rivals than a searching inquiry into how issues such as race could shape and control a society.

Yet by the start of the 1970s few issues would have more prominence or significance than the feminist revolution and the changes taking place in the everyday lives of countless women. It all happened because of the flowering of criticism and reform that came with the emergence of a new generation; ultimately, women's issues

Eleanor Roosevelt (second from left) leads a 1962 meeting of the President's Commission on the Status of Women at Valkill, her cottage in Hyde Park, New York.

could not be ignored once young people started to rebel against social norms, students began to challenge discrimination based on race (why not sex as well?), and antipoverty crusaders started to examine the roots of economic oppression. Questions of gender and sexual politics may not have been the headlines that seized popular attention in 1962, but they were just below the surface, ready to become the news story that, in the end, helped define an era.

No dramatic social change occurs for a single reason or springs from one group of people alone. But any effort to understand the transforming power of feminism in the late 1960s and 1970s has to begin with the young people who were attending college when John Kennedy was inaugurated. Those college students already reflected a dramatic shift in life patterns. Twenty years earlier, when their parents were their age, only 15 percent of American youth had gone to college. But then had come World War II, the emergence of a fast-paced economy fueled by consumer purchases, a housing boom and technological innovation, and a corresponding explosion of economic and educational opportunities.

The "affluent society" featured not only a mass migration of young families to suburbia, the proliferation of sprawling shopping malls, and huge growth in automobile ownership and highway construction. It also necessitated a system of higher education that mass-produced the scientists, managers, and technological experts to sustain and expand the gains that had been made. America had become a "knowledge" society, which made the university and its residents a central part of the nation's nervous system. Thus, by 1965 the proportion of young people attending college had exploded to 45 percent—three times the proportion of a quarter century earlier. Reflecting the integral connection between education and the affluent society, 75 percent of these college students came from families with incomes above the national median. They represented—and were expected to reproduce—the social and economic comfort from which they came.

Yet the experience of having grown up in such comfort also gave young people a different perspective from which to consider their lifetime goals and priorities. Their parents had been raised during the hardships of the Great Depression in the 1930s and the uncertainties of war in the 1940s. They had struggled to win economic

Natalie Wood and James Dean starred in Rebel Without a Cause, *a movie that captured the restlessness and quest for meaning of the younger generation.*

security and then prosperity in the postwar era. But for the younger generation, such material comfort was taken for granted, not a distant prize to be won or an elusive goal whose attainment would give life its meaning. Perhaps that was why James Dean was such a cult hero for 1950s teenagers, and the film *Rebel Without a Cause* such a powerful generational symbol. Perhaps it was precisely "a cause" that young affluent Americans were searching for.

When they got to college, moreover, many of these students found an environment that encouraged them to be skeptical and critical of the social standards and practices that prevailed in the middle class. This was an era when the most popular book in sociology was *The Lonely Crowd* by David Riesman, a searing account of how Americans seemed to care more about pleasing others in order to get ahead than about standing up for their convictions. History and other disciplines started to focus more attention on such issues as slavery and racism. Universities had been dismissed by critics in the 1950s as mindless mazes through which conformist students moved quietly, like trained rats, toward a predetermined goal. That stereotype had always been overdrawn, but now it became positively wrong as students in different places and in different ways sought new answers and better questions.

In Cambridge, Massachusetts, for example, a group of Baptist students came together to form what was called the Fetter Family. Composed of young people attending Boston-area colleges, the "Family" met on a regular basis to talk about witnessing to their faith and to arrive at a clear commitment about how their religious views should be translated into practice in their communities. Each month members of the group journeyed to a town or village in Massachusetts to "testify" to their faith, agreeing—by prearrangement—to take over the programs of a local church for a weekend and to be in charge of everything from the Sunday sermon to the youth group.

In 1961 the theme of the Fetter Family was "Jesus Christ, the Revolutionary." When they went out to suburban towns and wondered out loud what Jesus Christ, the Revolutionary, might have to say about real estate contracts that barred blacks from moving to decent housing, or moralistic codes that said boys could be sexually active but girls must remain virgins, they were expressing some of the new energy and social criticism that were bubbling to the surface on campuses throughout the country.

It was that kind of energy that received formal expression in 1962 when a group of students from throughout the country came together in Ann Arbor, Michigan, to offer their manifesto for the

A rally for the Free Speech Movement at the University of California at Berkeley. Berkeley was a center of student protest during much of the 1960s.

future. "We are the people of this generation," the Students for a Democratic Society (SDS) declared, "bred in at least moderate comfort, housed now in universities, looking uncomfortably to the world we inherit." Disturbed by the expectation that they should conform to the values and practices of their parents, they insisted on a larger perspective, critical of technocracy, committed to ending racial and social injustice, and devoted to building communities where people could live "with dignity and creativeness." Some of the young, at least, were ready to declare their agenda for change, and they believed they could achieve it.

A second place to look for the reasons why feminism and women's issues became so visible by the end of the decade is in the civil rights movement. No struggle shaped the 1960s generation as much as that of black Americans to secure full equality and justice. Nor did any other movement capture so completely the desire to create a better world. If white students were ready to criticize the world they inherited, the issue of racial discrimination offered them a powerful weapon; if they wished to act on their ideals and religious faith to show they could "make a difference," the cause of civil rights offered an ethical case in point to demonstrate their commitment; and if they hoped to find through their activism a real-life alternative to the world they were now questioning, there was no more inspiring model than that of the "beloved community" where blacks and whites, living and working together, could make peace and love and justice a reality.

The civil rights movement, of course, had its own long history, going back well before the 1940s and 1950s. Yet in its more recent existence, the movement provided particular themes and examples likely to inspire and galvanize the young. The first large-scale demonstration of black refusal to accept second-class treatment came in 1955 in Montgomery, Alabama, when Rosa Parks, a deeply respected member of the black community, was arrested for refusing to give up her seat on a city bus because a white person was standing while she was sitting. Four days after her arrest, Montgomery's black population declared a boycott of the city's bus line. Not a single African American rode to work on a public bus that day. When the boycott was extended, Montgomery's blacks stayed off the buses—for 381 days—until segregation on the bus system ended.

Their new spokesman, Martin Luther King, Jr., offered a rationale for their nonviolent protest. "There comes a time," King said, "when people get tired. We are here . . . to say to those who have mistreated us so long that we are tired—tired of being segregated and humiliated, tired of being kicked about by the brutal feet of oppression." But black Americans would not retaliate with anger or hatred. Rather, they would respond with sacrifice and love. "If you will protest courageously and yet with dignity and Christian love," King declared, "in the history books that are written in future generations, historians will have to pause and say, 'there lived a great people—a black people—who injected a new meaning and dignity into the veins of civilization.'"

Still another inspiration of the civil rights movement was that provided by students themselves—the four black freshmen (all men) in Greensboro, North Carolina, who sat in at the lunch counter of the local Woolworth's on February 1, 1960, and set in motion a revolution. These black students, like their white counterparts in the Fetter Family and the SDS, were coming to grips with the world they had inherited. They had become politically conscious in 1954, the same year the Supreme Court ruled in *Brown* v. *Board of Education* that segregation in public education was unconstitutional and must be ended. For six years the students had waited patiently for change to happen, as their parents petitioned the local school board, their ministers preached about justice, and their teachers taught them to aspire to greatness. Yet no changes had occurred. Now the students decided that they were the ones accountable for securing jus-

Rosa Parks, best known for her role in initiating the Montgomery, Alabama, bus boycott in 1955, continued to be an eloquent spokesperson for the cause of civil rights. A veteran of the NAACP, Parks became an especially important role model for younger blacks who learned about her courage in their elementary schools.

After the lunch counter sit-in at the Woolworth's in Greensboro, North Carolina, the dime-store chain became a nationwide target of protests against Jim Crow policies. This picket line was set up in Jamaica, Queens, in New York City.

tice. If they failed to act, they would become accomplices in evil, accepting the plague of American racism and being responsible for its perpetuation.

So on Monday afternoon on the first day of February, they went to downtown Greensboro. They bought school supplies and toiletries at counters where they were treated courteously. Then they went to the lunch counter, sat down, and ordered coffee. "We don't serve Negroes," the waitress said. "But we have receipts," the students responded. "We were served over there, and now we want to be served here." After three hours the store closed and the four students went back to the campus. Word spread of what they had done. The next morning 23 of their classmates joined them at the lunch counter, sitting there and studying all day, waiting for service, being taunted by angry whites. The third day there were 66, now both men and women; the fourth day, 100. And on the fifth day there were 1,000 students. Within two months the sit-ins had spread to 54 cities in 9 states.

In April 1960 men and women students from all over the South came together in Raleigh, North Carolina, to form the Student Non-Violent Coordinating Committee (SNCC). Its credo, similar to that of Dr. King, was a powerful evocation of the faith, confidence, and spirit that would inspire a generation. "We affirm the philosophical . . . ideal of non-violence as a foundation of our purpose," SNCC leader James Lawson declared, "the presupposition of our faith, and the manner of our action . . . Love is the central motif of non-violence . . . Such love goes to the extreme; it remains loving and forgiving even in the midst of hostility. It matches the capacity of evil to inflict suffering with an even more enduring capacity to absorb evil, all the while persisting in love." To people looking for an ideal to live and possibly die for, the SNCC credo embodied the best that America had to offer.

Although it was not noticed or commented upon very much at the time, many of the most important figures of leadership in the civil rights movement were women. Rosa Parks had long been a mainstay of the NAACP (National Association for the Advancement of Colored People) in Montgomery, dedicated to finding whatever means of protest could be used to fight discrimination and promote better treatment for blacks. The key individuals who organized the Montgomery bus boycott were members of the Women's Political Council, a voluntary association of black women interested in civic affairs. Led by Jo Ann Robinson, an English professor at Alabama State University, they had gone into action immediately through their "phone tree" to notify virtually everyone in the community of the action that was forthcoming. Ella Baker, a North Carolina native,

Ella Baker addresses a meeting of the Student Non-Violent Coordinating Committee (SNCC) in Hattiesburg, Mississippi, in January 1964. Baker was not only known as the "mother" of SNCC but she was also one of the few figures able to hold the group together when it entered its period of fragmentation after the Freedom Summer of 1964.

The bookkeepers at the State National Bank in Odessa, Texas, in 1954 were exclusively women; the managers were male.

was in many ways the mother of the civil rights movement. One of the NAACP's chief organizers in the South during the 1930s and 1940s, she had started the NAACP youth chapter in Greensboro that helped produce the sit-ins. She also served as the acting executive director of Martin Luther King, Jr.'s Southern Christian Leadership Conference at the end of the 1950s (male ministers, she found, were more comfortable making her "acting" director rather than director), and more than anyone else it was she who was responsible for SNCC becoming an independent group, free of control from any other civil rights organization. In Greensboro itself, a black schoolteacher, Nell Coley, had been a constant source of inspiration to the sit-in students, telling them "the way you find things need not happen . . . I don't care if they push and shove you, you must not accept [discrimination]. . . You are who you are."

As some white students came to join blacks in SNCC during the early 1960s, they would find other black women playing the pivotal roles in the movement. These roles demonstrated a new kind of possibility for women's activism, one not usually associated with the roles social convention prescribed for women. The realization of this possibility did not occur immediately, nor did it lead, like some mathematical formula, to a spontaneous new commitment to women's

Women with few skills often found work as supermarket checkers. In such jobs, they were able to work in their communities, close to their homes and children.

rights. But along with the movement itself, and the growing criticism of societal norms that was emerging in the new generation, this experience too would make a significant difference in the gradual emergence of a feminist agenda.

In the meantime, other less visible changes had been taking place over the preceding decades to make the legal and economic status of women a significant concern for policymakers. For most of the 20th century there had been a gradual expansion of the number of women in the labor force. Most of these women were young, single, and poor. They worked almost exclusively in sex-segregated jobs, such as domestic service and clerical positions. Where they did occupy jobs similar to those held by men, they were paid only a fraction of the male wage. A disproportionate number of women workers came from immigrant backgrounds or were African Americans or Latinas. Although over time more married women joined the labor force, especially during the depression when survival required that everyone earn money if possible, there remained a pervasive expectation that all but the poorest women should concentrate on homemaking once they married and started to have children.

Although World War II did not alter this situation overnight, it did accelerate some of the long-term trends in women's employment and changed the cultural dynamics affecting women's work. More than six million women took jobs during the labor crisis created by the war—an increase in the female labor force of more than 50 percent; but most important, 75 percent of these women were married and 60 percent were over the age of 35. With the end of the war came a massive propaganda campaign to force women to return to the home (more than 75 percent of the new workers said they wanted to retain their jobs), yet some effects of the wartime experience remained. The proportion of married women in the labor force had increased from 15 percent in 1940 to almost 25 percent in 1950. The average age of women workers had increased. And more and more women who were middle class and educated were taking jobs. No progress had been made on issues of sex equality, such as equal pay or access to high-paying jobs. But some changes of long-range importance were underway.

The aftermath of World War II produced a kind of cultural division in attitudes toward women. On the one hand, psychologists, family "experts," advertisers, and public opinion leaders embarked on a concerted campaign to celebrate domesticity. At a time when having children was seen as both patriotic and the key to domestic bliss, women's magazines portrayed mothers and housewives as "daily content in a world of bedroom, kitchen, sex, babies and home." A best-selling book, coauthored by a female psychiatrist, insisted that mental illness was the logical consequence of feminism and of women trying to be like men. "The independent woman," it declared, "is a contradiction in terms." Only when American women put out of their heads any idea of equality and reclaimed instead the arts of canning, cooking, and interior decorating could they find creative fulfillment. As if to confirm that the baby boom and domesticity were inextricably linked, the authors of *Modern Woman: The Lost Sex* (1947) concluded with the observation that women could find happiness only when they learned "to accept with deep inwardness and readiness . . . the final goal of [intercourse]—impregnation." According to these and other experts, women's highest calling and deepest satisfaction consisted of full-time devotion to the career of being good wives and mothers.

Yet at the same time that such lessons were flooding magazines like *McCall's* and TV comedies like "Father Knows Best," many

This ad for Maytag appliances promoted the concept of domestic bliss—a mother glowing with the pleasure of raising her children and of caring for the family's home.

women were acting in ways that seemed to contradict the experts' advice. All during the suburban bliss of the 1950s, women were taking jobs at a rate four times faster than men. Frequently, these were not full-time jobs. Rarely were they in fields where possibilities existed for promotion or high pay. Nor did there appear to be any "feminist" motivation driving women to the work force. In fact, women were taking jobs in order to help the family move one rung higher on the middle-class ladder, afford an addition to the suburban tract house they had just bought, set money aside for a college fund for the kids, or buy a new car. It was part of becoming a member of the affluent society.

Moreover, women—especially middle-class women—were developing a pattern of seeking jobs that had its own clear cultural logic. The greatest increase in employment among women took place among those over 35 whose children—ages 6 to 17—were in school. The proportion of women at work in that category leaped from 25 percent in 1950 to 39 percent in 1960. Thus young mothers were still staying at home, to do what the magazines said they should do, but they were taking jobs once their children started to go to school so that the family as a whole could enjoy a better life. By 1960 the percentage of married women at work had doubled compared to 1940 (from 15 percent to 30 percent), and both husbands and wives worked outside the home in more than 10 million families (an increase of 330 percent over 1940).

To an increasing extent, some economists and policymakers started to take note of these trends. The National Manpower Council, for example, conducted a lengthy study aimed at improving "development and utilization of the country's human resources." Published at the same time the Soviet Union seemed to be racing ahead of the United States in technology (*Sputnik,* the Soviet space satellite, had been launched in 1957, the world's first such venture), the council's book, *Womanpower,* emphasized that women's talents were essential to winning the competition for control of the world. According to one expert, data from college entrance examinations, administered by the Educational Testing Service, showed that women constituted 98 percent of the bright young people who did not go to

In the late 1950s and early 1960s the proportion of women working outside the home grew rapidly. A sizable number, like these auto workers, took jobs traditionally held by men.

college. Was it not time to look anew at the job opportunities available to women, the extent to which they were not receiving the training necessary to maximize their abilities, and the degree to which the government bore a responsibility to advance the status of women as a precious national resource?

It was against this backdrop that newly elected President John F. Kennedy appointed his national Commission on the Status of Women in 1961. In part he was paying off a political debt to Esther Peterson, a longtime supporter who for years had worked in the halls of Congress as a lobbyist for garment workers and other labor union women, and whom Kennedy now appointed head of the Women's Bureau of the U.S. Department of Labor. Kennedy also hoped to solidify his position with liberals, naming Eleanor Roosevelt to be the honorary chair of the commission. Hardly a bold or risky maneuver from Kennedy's point of view, examining the status of women seemed an ideal way to signal recognition of an important constituency and support for moving forward to mobilize the full resources of the country to win the Cold War.

In fact, the commission fulfilled Kennedy's hopes, completing in 1963 a comprehensive, balanced, and careful analysis of women's situation. It covered some important new ground on women's issues, emphasizing, for example, the critical importance of child care facilities to full utilization of women's resources, recommending paid

President Kennedy signs the Equal Pay Act in 1963. Among the witnesses were Esther Peterson (front row, left, in light dress), head of the Women's Bureau, and Vice President Lyndon B. Johnson (far right).

maternity leave, and supporting an extension of unemployment and minimum-wage benefits to large numbers of women previously uncovered. Perhaps most important, it focused attention on the pervasive inequities women experienced on the job, preparing the way for the Equal Pay Act of 1963. This act mandated that where women and men did exactly the same job, they should receive exactly the same wage.

On some of the more contentious issues it faced, the commission embraced compromise. Ever since 1923 the National Woman's Party, headed by Alice Paul, had singlemindedly pursued passage and ratification of the Equal Rights Amendment (ERA) to the Constitution, an amendment that would have prohibited any law that used sex as a basis for treating men and women differently. The problem was that most women's organizations all the way up to the 1960s believed that some legislation protecting women was necessary. Widow's pension laws, regulations governing night work, provisions limiting the amount of weight a woman could be asked to carry—all these laws would be abolished under the ERA. Although after 1941 the Supreme Court ruled that minimum-wage and maximum-hour laws could be extended to men as well as women (previously, the Court had said only women could be protected), many women reformers were still convinced that some laws recognizing women's differences were useful. They believed the primary purpose of the ERA was to promote a reactionary, hands-off policy designed to free businesses from any obligation to treat women fairly.

Isola Dodie had been working for women's rights for nearly 70 years when she took part in the National Era Countdown Campaign in 1981.

When confronted with this long-simmering controversy, the commissioners, in effect, agreed to disagree. Their final report declared that the ERA "need not now be sought," advocating instead another strategy for promoting women's legal rights. The 14th Amendment to the Constitution guaranteed all citizens "equal protection under the law," and the commission believed that this clause could serve as a basis for freeing women citizens from discriminatory treatment—much in the same way that black civil rights advocates had used it.

Yet the commission's most important contribution was not what it said or failed to say, but the fact that it existed. It gave formal acknowledgment to the fact that women's rights and opportunities were of critical national importance. The commission had gathered information and made recommendations, but of even greater significance, it created an organizational structure of people sharing common concerns. These people were committed to working together to develop a common base of data from which to proceed.

To use a word that later would become synonymous with this phenomenon, a "network" had been established. Pivotal to that network were a series of state commissions on the status of women. These commissions were created throughout the country to pursue on a local level the same work being done by the national commission. Starting in 1964, that network of state commissions gathered annually in Washington, D.C., to assess the progress that had been made on women's agenda of change and to generate collective strategies for the next step. It was precisely such a gathering that in 1966 would lead to a result that John F. Kennedy could never have anticipated in 1961—creation of a National Organization for Women (NOW), which would become the civil rights vanguard of a reborn and revitalized feminism.

Many concerns were on the minds of the politicians who were preparing to take power in the winter of 1961 as representatives of the "new generation of Americans," but it is unlikely that a single one of those individuals saw women's rights, child care, or gender roles as priority issues. These men, after all, were "technocrats" who prided themselves on "crisis management," "fine-tuning" the economy, and calibrating the most efficient strategy for containing the spread of communism. Yet historical change often comes from unantici-

The founding members of NOW posed for this historic photograph in 1966. Betty Friedan is at center.

pated consequences as well as from well-planned designs. Whatever the actual priorities of the Kennedy administration, its leaders and participants conveyed a message of change, of vitality, of confidence, and of commitment. "We can do better," the President said.

To a degree that he would never have been aware of in advance, that sense of commitment—the feeling that people could make a difference—resonated with undercurrents that had already begun to be felt throughout the society. The whole history of postwar America had been dominated by change, yet the cultural impression in place at the end of the 1950s was of complacency, conformity, and comfort. Many segments of the society were prepared to burst that bubble and address some of the contradictions and inequities that for too long had lingered beneath the surface.

Thus the rise of John Kennedy and the transition it represented became primarily a symbol of the country being ready to face new problems. Kennedy himself might care most about conducting wars of national liberation in Vietnam or Africa and facing down the Soviet Union, but young people heard his call for a Peace Corps the loudest. Those who joined could go and help someone in a developing country to find a better life. The administration's civil rights policies were initially designed to put a lid on civil rights protests and keep the President from being embarrassed when he went abroad.

President Kennedy greets a crowd of Peace Corps trainees at the White House as they trained for their overseas assignments. The Peace Corps became a national symbol of the youth and optimism of the Kennedy years.

But their effect was to deepen and accelerate the determination of black and white activists to make the American revolution happen at home.

In the end it was those who received and interpreted the messages of change rather than those who pronounced them who would make the greatest difference in the nation's social history. By the end of the Kennedy administration young people, civil rights activists, and women reformers had all given their own meaning to the phrase "We can do better." Before too long, it would be clear that a common thread running through each reading of the phrase was the need to take seriously the issue of equality between women and men in America.

A WOMAN WITHOUT A MAN IS LIKE A FISH WITHOUT A BICYCLE

CHAPTER 2

DIFFERENT AUDIENCES

L ate in the 1970s a bumper sticker began to appear regularly on cars owned by feminists. It read: "A Woman Without a Man Is Like a Fish Without a Bicycle." The interpretation of the phrase could be as varied as the individuals reading it. But one clear message was that women could survive and prosper without men to clutter up their environment, just as fish could survive and prosper without bicycles. Men and women were of different worlds, with different rhythms, attributes, priorities, and values. In short, they had little if anything to do with each other.

That was a radical message, light-years away from where young students and civil rights workers were in the early 1960s. It would take multiple stages of alienation, anger, and bitterness before such a bumper sticker could emerge. In the meantime, events had to unfold, and a thousand different voices had to be heard. The overpowering irony of the idea of a woman's movement was that women were everywhere, constituting 51 percent of the population, members of all classes and of all ethnic, religious, political, and economic groups. If, as some argued, women were oppressed like minorities, they surely did not all share the same material circumstances, suffer the same degree of discrimination, or live together in the same run-

In the 1960s and 1970s, people wore their opinions on their shirts. The curious logic of this one also made its way onto bumper stickers as it punctured traditional assumptions of women's dependence on men.

down neighborhoods as some African Americans did on Chicago's South Side or as Mexican Americans did in the Los Angeles barrios. What, then, did it mean to share an identity? Did a rich, white, college-educated woman who ran the local Junior League have more in common with her Latina maid who had never gone to high school than with her rich, white, college-educated husband? What defined the bonds of gender? And could they be as strong as the bonds of class or ethnicity or religion?

Ultimately, any movement that developed to address issues of gender inequality had to deal with the question of audience. If a woman without a man was like a fish without a bicycle, it was even more true that a cause without a public to support it was no cause at all. Who, then, were some of the potential audiences among women in the early 1960s that might follow this movement if it came into being? What were their concerns? How ready were they to join a larger political and social revolution? What mattered to them? And were they prepared to share their individual discontents and find in that sharing the basis for collective action based on a common identity?

At least in retrospect, the most striking thing women appeared to have in common in the early 1960s was a sense of relative happi-

Suburban women dressed up in pearls and high heels to attend Tupperware parties, where they eagerly purchased housewares from their neighborhood sales representative. Such sales meetings also served as social occasions for women whose entire lives were focused on home and family.

ness. In 1962 the George Gallup polling organization asked a cross section of American women whether they were content with their lot. Two out of three women said yes. When the question was posed whether women as a group were victims of inequality or discrimination, only one in three women said yes. From one perspective, of course, that level of discontent was very high, suggesting profound problems. On the other hand, the overall level of satisfaction seemed high, especially in light of other polls in which most women said the greatest fulfillment of their lives was when they gave birth to their children, and a strong majority expressed satisfaction with their roles as homemakers.

One way to read such evidence is to conclude that some, and perhaps many, women did have problems in their lives but that they saw these problems as peculiar to themselves or their own circumstances, not as part of a shared phenomenon based on their being women. Thus they might reflect on their individual family situation, even talk about it with their women friends, and still not see their dilemma as a "woman" problem. In the early 1960s there was not yet even a label for such concerns. As feminist author Betty Friedan would later describe it, it was a "problem that had no name." Moreover, there was more than one problem—or at least the problem seemed different depending on who you were, how old you were, where you lived, and what you wanted. It was hard to discern unity in the face of such diversity. It was also important to understand how real women, in different circumstances, might perceive the world around them as it did or did not, from their point of view, reflect issues of gender. The experiences described here, and later, are those of real people, although their names and some details have been altered.

Laura Whiting was the daughter of English immigrants who came to America in 1903. She was born in 1913. Her father was a night watchman, her mother a cafeteria worker. Bright and energetic, Laura did well in high school. She then went on to take secretarial courses that enabled her to move beyond the occupational level of her parents and get a good clerical position by the time she was in her early 20s. She married on the eve of World War II, had a child within a year, and settled in comfortably to the role of wife and homemaker.

Laura's husband came from a slightly better background economically than she did, but he too had taken just a few business

courses after high school. Older than she, he did not have to go to fight in World War II but worked in a munitions plant instead. When the war was over he took a job as a bookkeeper, earning less than $3,000 a year. The couple rented an apartment and lived on a tight budget, but they worried about money. Eventually he inherited a house, but their budget remained tight, and it was sometimes a strain to find the extra money for new curtains or a vacation trip. With her child now in school most of the day, Laura wanted to go back to work, remembering fondly her job as a secretary and the social pleasures that came from chatting with other employees and making jokes.

But Laura's husband resisted that idea, refusing to give her permission to find a job, even part-time. He was somewhat old-fashioned, and believed that earning an income and providing for the family was a man's role. If she went to work, people might think he was not able to fill that role, that he was not really a man.

Laura went along with her husband's wishes. In the 1950s most people still believed in the sexual division of labor and man's authority in the family. But the disagreement between them was painful and sometimes bitter. She shared her unhappiness with some of her woman friends. They were all part of a woman's club at the church and would get together regularly to cook church suppers,

A group of Indiana women, members of Altrusa, a community service organization, hang a benefit art exhibit. Both full-time mothers and women with paid jobs outside the home made major contributions to their communities through such volunteer organizations.

run rummage sales, or have a monthly social at one of their homes. With her best friends in the group, Laura would discuss her concerns and in turn listen to their problems. Occasionally, the whole group would talk about family problems and men, sharing a common sensibility about the "war between the sexes." But no one ever uttered the word "feminism," and all the women seemed to feel the situation was perfectly normal. After all, every married couple had problems, and over time, they usually worked out.

In Laura's case, she eventually was able to persuade her husband that it was all right for her to take a part-time job, especially once their son was in college. She enjoyed the work and the people enormously. She had been right. There was a zest and vitality that came from being out in the world. But she had still not made any connection in her own mind between the problem that she had experienced and larger issues that related to gender. She had solved her own problem, as others of her friends had solved theirs, and there did not seem to be a larger, overriding issue.

Hilda Newberry was born in 1930, 17 years after Laura, just as the Great Depression was beginning. Although Laura's father was out of work for a number of years, Hilda's family survived the economic crisis fairly well. A product of an old-stock upper New York

State family, she grew up in middle-class comfort. Because of her background and the expectations middle-class families had for their daughters in those days, Hilda went to an excellent private junior college for women at the end of the 1940s. The intellectual content of the courses was solid. But in the ordinary course of events, students went there to acquire the kind of education that would prepare them for a brief work career and then marriage to a professional or business person of comparable background.

That was what happened to Hilda. In the early 1950s she fell in love with the son of an advertising executive. After she accompanied him on a brief stint in the army, they settled down in New York, where he began a career in business. He soon became a banker on Wall Street, and with growing success, earned enough so that they could move to a suburb on Long Island. Different from the new mass-produced tract house suburbs, such as Levittown, their town did not have concentric circles of boxlike houses. Instead, there were older, tree-lined streets on a more rectangular plan. But the houses were still very close together.

Ordinarily, the mothers gathered to keep an eye on the young children, to share gossip, and to have fun. In these backyard get-togethers there was always news to share—whose husband was getting what promotion, the latest addition to the neighborhood, emotional or physical problems among the children. It was also a place

A weekend softball game involves several generations. Suburban sports activities, though organized for the children, also provided social opportunities for their parents.

where you could talk about your private hopes and dreams or the difficulties you were having in your marriage. Sometimes the conversation would even touch on such topics as sex and divorce. The women formed a close-knit community, solidified each day by shared rituals of coffee, conversation, and child supervision. They were dedicated on one level simply to helping each other get through the day but, in an even larger sense, to building and maintaining the family as a unit and the community as a group enterprise.

It became fashionable in the late 1950s and early 1960s to denounce suburbia. For example, the suburbs, architectural critic Lewis Mumford declared, consisted of a "multitude of uniform, unidentifiable houses, lined up inflexibly, at uniform distances, in a treeless communal wasteland, inhabited by people of the same class, the same income, the same age group." But such indictments all too frequently ignored the human dramas of creativity and tragedy that were occurring daily. Weekly neighborhood barbecues or church "family" nights might seem to intellectual skeptics to be artificial substitutes for community, but to many of the participants they provided the space within which important bonds could be forged, friendships nurtured, and a sense of identity created.

In all this, women played the key roles. Some of Hilda's friends took part-time jobs at the local library and public school. Others devoted long hours to volunteer work with the PTA, Cub Scouts,

Many mothers volunteered as leaders of Girl Scout troops, conveying to their daughters the ideals of voluntarism and community service.

and Brownies. Most spent endless hours in the activities so often caricatured in novels and high-brow magazines—chauffeuring children to ballet lessons and Little League practice and driving their husbands to and from the commuter train station. But for the most part, suburban women's days were neither mindless nor empty. In an outward extension of the spirit that animated their backyard conversations, they were giving substance and purpose to a way of life.

Often Hilda and her friends also shared their feelings of anger and alienation about this way of life. Like the college graduates whom Betty Friedan wrote about in *The Feminine Mystique* (1963), they felt that their education and talents had been put on the shelf before

As she traveled throughout the country to promote the ideas in her groundbreaking book The Feminine Mystique, *Betty Friedan urged American women to reexamine their lives.*

even being tried out in the real world. Their days took on a uniformity that discouraged the flowering of individual interests and skills. A person trained in design, literature, or political science could well feel that she had entered a time warp upon getting married and moving to suburbia—shut off totally from the life and excitement she had once known.

There were also the problems that came with compartmentalized sex roles—husbands in work situations full of managerial crises, occasional flirtations, and at least the appearance of worldly sophistication; wives frustrated by the inability to have shared experiences to discuss at dinnertime. Where was the partnership everyone talked about in this age of "companionate" marriage? How did people share a life when their existence was so separate and different? And what about the expectations of her? Why did she always change the diapers and do the laundry? What was her goal, her objective, to reach? He had his career and the next big law case to spur him on. What did she have, especially when, at the occasional business dinner, she was expected to discuss babies and recipes with the other wives and not to challenge the pomposity of her husband's colleague on subjects she knew far more about than he?

Thus the conversations in the backyard and over coffee represented a confluence of concerns. On good days, the sense of fellowship, affection—yes, even sisterhood, though that word had not yet become part of a political vocabulary—made the life of community building in the suburbs seem rewarding and self-justifying. On bad days the frustration over the lack of companionship in marriage and the lack of opportunity for achievement and self-expression made the project of living on Long Island more a "suburban captivity," as one sociologist called it, than an exercise in creativity. For Hilda the good days outnumbered the bad. But then, in the early 1960s, there was still no language available to give a label to the moments of discontent or to define them as part of a collective experience rather than as isolated and temporary phenomena. Whether that language, once developed, spoke to her life and concerns in ways she could respond to would have a great deal to do with the success or failure of any woman's movement.

Barbara Harris had a life very different from that of either Hilda Newberry or Laura Whiting. Born toward the end of World War II,

Betty Friedan and her daughter Emily. Friedan's feminist views were rooted in her own experience as a Smith-educated journalist who had temporarily given up her professional activities to raise her family.

she was the fourth daughter in an African-American family that eventually included eight children. Her father had migrated to Winston-Salem from Warren County, North Carolina, where his family raised tobacco on a 30-acre farm. In 1930 Winston-Salem was a fast-growing, "new South" city where life was supposedly better for black people. He became a tobacco stemmer in the R. J. Reynolds cigarette factory, and his wife worked as a part-time domestic servant, cleaning the homes of white people five or six hours each day.

Their daughter Barbara was bright, funny, and very pretty. Like her mother, she became active in the local AME Zion Church, singing in the youth choir, going to prayer meetings, helping with the food preparation and service at the wonderful meals that always seemed to highlight religious gatherings. She felt very well off, at least relative to some of her friends, until her father suddenly left home after his eighth child had been born. From that time on he would pop up periodically in their lives, but he was no longer a stable presence, financially or otherwise.

When it came time for Barbara to go to high school in 1958, there was already talk about demanding that blacks be able to en-

Black citizens picket the school board office in St. Louis, Missouri, in 1963. Segregation was still rampant in the North as well as the South, as were picket lines protesting such policies.

roll at previously all-white schools. Some of Barbara's friends petitioned to do so in accordance with the Supreme Court's *Brown* decision, which had mandated an end to segregation, but the process was long and painful and often meant harassment and intimidation from whites. Barbara's mother could not afford the time or trouble that such a struggle entailed, and so Barbara went to the all-black high school that her older sisters had attended. But Barbara was very aware of segregation and the growing talk about challenging it. Every time she climbed up to the balcony of the downtown theater to sit in the "colored" section, she thought about the issue.

When Barbara was 16, in her junior year, the sit-ins began in nearby Greensboro. One week later they broke out at Woolworth's in Winston-Salem. The sit-in was led by Carl Matthews, a friend of her oldest sister. She and her classmates were thrilled and frightened. Here was a group of students, hardly older than they were, taking on the entire system of racism—defying all those white policemen, refusing to leave the five-and-dime when ordered to by the manager, sitting there and being spat upon and sworn at by all those white kids with their leather jackets and slicked-back hair. Then one day a classmate of Barbara's suggested that a group of high school students go down to Woolworth's and join the demonstrations. After all, he said, they were part of the new generation too. Why shouldn't they do their part?

Barbara was terrified, but she also was excited. This was the chance of a lifetime, an opportunity to change her life and that of everyone else she knew with black skin. She did not tell her mother about her plans, because she knew she would be worried. But with her other high school classmates, Barbara went downtown the next day after school and took her place at the lunch counter alongside all those other college and high school students who were insisting that life be different and better. It was the greatest moment she had ever experienced.

Barbara was smart enough and had good enough grades to go on to college or a technical institute after high school. But in her senior year she met a boy and fell in love. A few months later she discovered that she was pregnant. It was 1961, abortion was not something that people talked about very much, and, besides, having a child was a source of pride and achievement. Barbara had thought about what it would be like to become a civil rights worker in Mississippi or Georgia—like the students she saw on television, demonstrating, being beaten, sometimes being murdered. But now she had a daughter and had to find some way to support her.

As the years went by, Barbara's life did not become any easier. She took a job as a receptionist at an insurance company. She eventually married and had another child. But the relationship was not smooth. Her husband went out with other women, and when she complained, he hit her. After five years he moved out, leaving her to support the children alone. Some of her other women friends had the same kind of problem, and they talked about it together.

On the one hand, so many things seemed to be changing for the better. There was now a civil rights law, passed in 1964, that abolished the separate eating, bathroom, and theater facilities; and a voting rights act, passed in 1965, gave every black person the right to vote. Yet Barbara and most of her friends were still barely able to survive on a paycheck not much more than the minimum wage. Barbara thought about how good it would be if she had a husband who loved her and could help support the children, and she sometimes wondered whether this problem between women and men was universal and whether anything could be done about it. But usually she worried more about putting enough food on the table and buying

President Lyndon B. Johnson signs the Voting Rights Act of 1965. In the front row were his wife, Lady Bird, Attorney General Robert F. Kennedy (sixth from right), Senator Hubert Humphrey (fourth from right) and Speaker of the House John McCormack (far right). Martin Luther King, Jr., is directly behind Johnson in the second row.

winter coats for the kids. The rest seemed almost like a given, the way things were, something you could not really change.

In important ways the stories of Laura Whiting, Hilda Newberry, and Barbara Harris exemplify the diversity of experience and background that women brought to the early 1960s. They were of different ages, different economic classes, different races and religions. Anyone who talked to them about their daily lives would, in all likelihood, be impressed mainly by how distinctive their life histories were. Each was a product of her own time, place, and background. If they had met, each would have been fascinated most by how different her own perspectives and concerns were from those of the others.

Yet these women were united as well by common experiences shaped by their gender. They may not have used such a word in 1962—at least in the way it came to be used two decades later—but the reality of their lives reflected some shared concerns. To begin with, all grew up in a culture that, notwithstanding class and ethnic differences, assigned individuals different roles based on their sex. Women were always expected to do the housework, care for the children, and cook the meals; where men were part of their lives, women were also expected to follow their lead and be deferential. No matter what a woman's race, class, or religion, she was limited

Black women typically found work in service occupations such as kitchen work. Despite some progress in the hiring of black women for clerical and sales positions, there was still a tendency to force black women to take these lower-paying jobs.

Child care was women's work not just in cities and suburbs but also on farms. This woman juggles baby and farm equipment as she bears her dual responsibilities.

to certain kinds of jobs, ordinarily segregated by sex, which paid lower wages and had fewer opportunities for promotion than those held by men.

Perhaps the most important bond uniting women was the nature of their personal relationship to men. The details of individual women's lives might vary enormously, but common to their experience was the difficulty of negotiating and living with men accustomed to privilege, control, and power based on their sex. For Barbara Harris it might mean being hit; for Laura Whiting, being told she could not take a job; for Hilda Newberry, being expected to keep her mouth shut when one of her husband's colleagues said something stupid. But in each case there was a boundary that represented a territorial difference potentially far greater than any that might divide the three women from each other.

There was also the opportunity, shared by each of these women, to confide in their sisters—women from the same class, background, or neighborhood whom they knew in many ways far more intimately than they did the men in their lives. These women shared a common language, a common set of experiences, and common priorities—at least within their own culture. Whether it was Hilda in the backyard, Laura at the church supper, or Barbara with her high school classmates, a community existed that offered a sounding board, reinforcement, and emotional sustenance.

The key question was whether these ties of commonality were strong and flexible enough to prevail over the erosive powers of difference. Despite the similarities that women shared by virtue of having to deal with men, they had to face the realization that these were at least *their* men—of the same class, ethnic group, and religion—not someone else's men. The sex one was born into could easily be the most decisive part of an individual's identity. Masculinity and femininity, after all, represented labels almost as strong and binding as any that one could imagine.

But was gender as powerful a source of identity as race? Given a choice of which was more important in her life, would Barbara Harris select the gender she had in common with Hilda Newberry, or the color she shared with her husband? If one woman was poor and worked on a factory floor with other poor people, male and female, did she have more in common with them, or with the wife of the factory owner, who was rich?

Whatever their different backgrounds, Laura Whiting, Hilda Newberry, and Barbara Harris each had identified a problem in their lives having to do with men. For every one of them in the early 1960s, it was a "problem that has no name." They talked about it with each other, they described similar situations, but they all saw their predicaments as individual in nature, part of "the way things are," dilemmas to be coped with, each woman by herself.

The issue for the future was what would happen when someone gave the problem a name, described its origins and development, and sought to forge a collective voice of protest and action to solve it. When that happened, which would prevail—the voice of commonality, or the voices of difference?

THE REBIRTH OF FEMINISM

During the 1960s, events sometimes happened so quickly that they almost seemed to outpace the speed of sound. In the fall of 1961 coeducational colleges still had what were called parietal rules regulating the few short periods of the week when men could be in woman's dorms and vice versa. Boys wore ties and button-down shirts and sported "whiffle" haircuts (so short that if you rubbed your hand over the bristles you could generate static electricity); girls wore skirts, starched blouses, knee socks, and pony tails. No one would think of calling a university president a derogatory name or breaking into official files.

By 1969, in contrast, rules had become synonymous with fascism. Male and female students lived with each other in the same dormitory room; a new sexual revolution had swept the country, accompanied by widespread experimentation with drugs. At the legendary rock festival at Woodstock in 1969, thousands of people gathered in open fields to hear their favorite musicians, celebrating not only a triumphant counterculture but brazenly flaunting conventional, middle-class behavior. Boys and girls wore jeans patched with fragments of the American flag, smoking marijuana was commonplace, and hair reached the lower backs of men and women alike. Policemen were routinely called "pigs" by some of the best

A leader of the women's liberation movement at the University of Michigan reads a manifesto that uses angry and often explicit language. Student protests against university administrations, a tactic used in the antiwar movement, expanded to include issues of women's and minority rights.

CHAPTER 3

This 1966 article from the National Insider, *a Chicago newspaper, reported on the changing sexual mores on college campuses. Not long afterward, many colleges not only liberalized visiting rules but some even instituted coed dorms.*

College Couples Demand The Right To Visit In Bedrooms

and brightest college students, and one university president, whose office was occupied by demonstrators, received a manifesto telling him: "up against the wall, mother-fucker." It was quite a decade.

In all of this turmoil, nothing changed more quickly, or posed so great a challenge to traditional authority and customs, as the ways some women thought of themselves and their role in society. In 1962 *Harper's Magazine* thought it was being bold in commenting that American women seemed "ardently determined to extend their vocation beyond the bedroom, kitchen and nursery." The editors could not have conceived of the possibility that a few short years later the daughters of some of these same women would demand the abolition of their confinement to the bedroom, kitchen, and nursery, an end to the traditional family, abortion "on demand," and—in some cases—the creation of all-female communities.

Even "moderate" feminists held sit-ins at the editorial offices of *Newsweek* and the *Ladies' Home Journal,* demanding that women be assured an equitable share of high-level positions. It was a time of extraordinary transformations, from dramatizing the "sexploitation" of the Miss America contest in 1968 to creating the legal and cultural framework to admit women to the military academies at West Point and Annapolis as equals with men.

When the leaders of President Kennedy's Commission on the Status of Women wrote their final report in 1963 demanding equal pay for equal work and an end to discriminatory treatment of women in the legal system and on the job, they were making a natural rights argument as old as the Declaration of Independence. Individuals possessed God-given rights, they emphasized, and it was a violation of universal laws of nature for these to be denied on the basis of such group characteristics as race or sex. As early as the 1940s, when the Carnegie Foundation issued its clarion call, authored by the Swedish sociologist Gunnar Myrdal, to end racial discrimination, sociologists and lawyers had commented that women were examples of an "American Dilemma." Like black people, they were members of a society committed to liberty and personal freedom, yet treated as separate and different because of a shared physical characteristic. The contradiction was profound, striking at the heart of the integrity of the American Creed. Only when all citizens were freed from such categorical discrimination could the American dream be considered workable.

Pauli Murray, a black lawyer who had pioneered the effort to get blacks admitted to Southern law schools in the 1930s, zeroed in

The swimsuit competition was the epitome of the Miss America contest's emphasis on women as sex objects. In 1968 members of the National Women's Liberation Movement demonstrated outside the pageant in Atlantic City, New Jersey, on the grounds that it set false goals for women.

Black lawyer and feminist Pauli Murray, who helped lead the fight to ensure women's equality before the law, recognized the similarities between race and sex discrimination. She encountered sexism as a student at Howard University Law School and recalled that it was the place "where I first became conscious of the twin evil of discriminatory sex bias."

on the connection between race and sex in her work for the Kennedy Commission on the Status of Women. Like black civil rights activists, she declared, women should prosecute their case for freedom by going to court and demanding that they be given equal protection under the laws, a right conferred by the 14th Amendment when in 1867 it sought to ensure the legal standing of the newly freed slaves by defining their citizenship rights. At the time Congress had inserted the word "male" in front of "citizen," temporarily caving in to those who still wanted to exclude women from fundamental rights, such as voting. But the 19th Amendment had altered that pattern when it recognized women's right to vote, and now, Murray argued, women should insist on carrying their case forward on the basis of the civil rights they enjoyed with all citizens under the clause of the 14th Amendment that declared, "No State shall ... deny to any person within its jurisdiction the equal protection of the laws."

Betty Friedan elaborated on the analogy in her 1963 book, *The Feminine Mystique,* and at the same time reached out to galvanize the consciousness of millions of American women by giving a label to "the problem that has no name." The dominant institutions of American culture, Friedan charged, had tried to treat women like children by enclosing them in "comfortable concentration camps" where they were told they must be happy because they were women, not individuals. Assigned a set of responsibilities solely on the basis of their sex, women had been denied the chance to cultivate their individual talents or assert their personal rights.

"I've tried everything women are supposed to do," one young mother wrote Friedan, "hobbies, gardening, pickling, canning, and being very social with my neighbors. . . . But I'm desperate. I begin to feel that I have no personality. I'm a server of food and putter-on of pants and a bedmaker, somebody who can be called on when you want something. But who am I?" The question struck at the heart of all the concerns that produced distress in the lives of Laura Whiting, Hilda Newberry, and Barbara Harris. They were always supposed to accept a man's commands, to fulfill some role society said was theirs, and forbidden to claim their own voice and challenge the status quo.

In the strange way that history happens, the actual direct linkage of the two causes came through a perverse attempt by an enemy of black civil rights to derail the 1964 Civil Rights Act. Representative Howard Smith, a conservative Southern Democrat, thought he could ensure defeat of the bill if he added women to its coverage, making sex—like race—susceptible to civil rights legislation. That idea was so ridiculous, Smith believed, that no one would support it, and the civil rights bill would fail to pass. But instead, an unusual coalition of conservatives and liberals formed to enact the amendment. It made perfect sense to outlaw discrimination against individuals because of their sex as well as the color of their skin, and women's rights activists had long understood the analogy. Now that logic was translated into the law as well, and it became a major instrument for achieving the goals of the President's Commission on the Status of Women.

On the other hand, it soon became clear that many of those responsible for enforcing the new legislation shared the opinion of Congressman Smith that adding women to the measure was more a joke than a serious public policy. Explicitly and implicitly, those charged with directing the Equal Employment Opportunities Commission (EEOC)—the government agency charged with implementing the civil rights law—gave notice that they would not treat complaints about sex discrimination the same way they would treat grievances based on racial discrimination. Once that policy was known, however, the network of women reformers that had formed around the President's commission went into action. Meeting in Washington, D.C., in 1966 to monitor enforcement provisions by the EEOC, members of the various state commissions on the status of women— led by Pauli Murray and Betty Friedan—decided the time had come, in Friedan's words, "to take the actions needed to bring women into the mainstream of American society, now, full equality for women, in fully equal partnership with men. NOW. The National Organization for Women."

With the formation of NOW in the fall of 1966, America's women's rights activists had an organization comparable to the NAACP, ready to fight through the media, the courts, and the Congress for the same rights for women that the NAACP sought for blacks. NOW focused on an "equal partnership of the sexes" in job opportunities, education, household responsibilities, and government. Friedan and her allies pressured President Johnson to include women

A meeting of the National Organization for Women (NOW) in 1966. Among the founders were Pauli Murray (fifth from left) and Betty Friedan (far right).

in his affirmative action policies, which were designed to hasten recruitment of minorities to decent jobs, and to appoint feminists to administrative and judicial offices. NOW endorsed the Equal Rights Amendment and made reform of abortion laws a national priority.

Equally important was the connection made by some young women between the treatment they received within the civil rights movement itself and the treatment blacks received from the larger society. Most of the young people in the early civil rights movement were black, but a significant minority were white, many of them women, including Sondra Cason (later Casey Hayden) from the Faith and Life community in Austin, Texas, and Mary King, daughter of a Protestant minister. Most of the younger activists joined the Student Non-Violent Coordinating Committee (SNCC), which created an atmosphere in which independent thinking and social criticism could flourish.

A new sense of empowerment infused the participants in civil rights activities, women and men alike. "If you are spending your time [doing] community organization, . . . opening people's awareness to their own power in themselves," Mary King noted, "it inevitably strengthens your own conceptions, your own ability." As women took their turn risking life and limb to make the movement happen, they were transformed in their own sense of who they were and what they could do. "I learned a lot of respect for myself for having gone through all of that," one said.

White women in particular were impressed by the black women they met. Some of them were older, those that black minister Charles

The work of the Congress of Racial Equality (CORE) drew on the talents of whites as well as blacks, who participated in voter registration drives and the Freedom Rides on interstate buses. The sign at left refers to the 1964 murders of three civil rights workers—including two whites, Andrew Goodman and Michael Schwerner—in Philadelphia, Mississippi.

Sherrod, the organizer of SNCC's project in southwest Georgia, called the "mommas" of the movement. "She is usually a militant woman in the community," Sherrod said, "outspoken, understanding, and willing to catch hell, having already caught her share." Fannie Lou Hamer of Mississippi was one of those. Evicted from her land for daring to register to vote, then beaten horribly by a white sheriff, she refused to give in to hate or fear. "Black and white together," she would sing out at civil rights rallies. "We are not afraid." Observing the effect Hamer had on people, the white volunteer Sally Belfrage observed that "a sort of joy began to grow in every face.... For just that second, no one is afraid, because they are free."

Younger black women exhibited some of the same strength and determination. Diane Nash was a Fisk University beauty queen, but what struck her colleagues in the movement was her quiet courage as she insisted on continuing the 1961 Freedom Rides through the South. These courageous bus trips tested the right of blacks to ride interstate buses with whites, in the face of wanton beatings from white thugs armed with steel pipes. In most of the activities SNCC conducted, women played a major role, demonstrating in action—not theory—that when it came to daring, boldness, and courage, they were the equals of any man.

On the other hand, some of the women also detected a typical

Diane Nash (second from right), a student at Fisk University, eats at the previously segregated lunch counter of the bus terminal in Nashville, Tennessee. One of the most courageous members of the Freedom Ride team of 1961, Nash subsequently became a leader of the Student Non-Violent Coordinating Committee.

male paternalism in the movement. Ella Baker had seen it when black male ministers adamantly refused to acknowledge her authority and talent by giving her the formal title of executive secretary of the Southern Christian Leadership Conference. Women in SNCC saw it when they were treated as though it was natural that they should do the typing and clerical work, or make the coffee, or take notes at meetings. "The attitude around here toward keeping the house neat," one volunteer said, "as well as the general attitude toward the inferiority and 'proper place' of women is disgusting."

To a large extent, these sentiments were held mainly by white women. Ironically, the movement—including the prominent role played by black women—had heightened their awareness and consciousness about being treated as less than equal. Precisely because the ideals of the "beloved community" were so high, any failure to measure up to those ideals became a crushing blow. Most black women in the movement seemed not to have the same response. They were already a part of the black community, they assumed their leadership roles in a natural and unforced manner, and they had other priorities. White women, on the other hand, were by definition less secure in their sense of identity within the movement, and therefore were potentially more critical.

The sense of alienation grew during Freedom Summer 1964, when nearly a thousand white volunteers came to Mississippi to join the black struggle and work for voter registration and better schools and health facilities for blacks. It was a summer of extraordinary tension and turmoil. Three civil rights workers were lynched—two of them white, one black. Scores of churches were torched by white terrorists after being used for voter registration rallies. Fear was rife, as bombs were thrown at "freedom houses" where SNCC women and men lived, and shotgun fire rang out regularly in the night. Interracial fissures grew within the movement as well. Black leaders resented white Northern liberals deigning to tell *them* what to do, while some Northern whites were distressed that their talents were not fully utilized.

It was relations between the sexes that provided the greatest trouble of all, however. At a time when a new sexual revolution was just getting underway, the old rules and regulations about whom you slept with and after how long no longer seemed so clear. This was compounded by the realization that the biggest social taboo of all—interracial sex—was one of the most suspect and oppressive of all those rules and regulations. If the goal of the movement was a truly beloved community, why not extend that to sexual interaction? And how better to show that you meant what you said about integration than to sleep with someone of the other race? Especially in the heat of what seemed like combat conditions, reaching out for love, or even just release, appeared to be a logical and perhaps politically inspired thing to do.

In reality, however, too many women (and some men) became sexual objects. Having intercourse could become a rite of passage imposed against one's will as well as a natural expression of bonding and affection. White and black women in particular became suspicious of each other, black women sometimes torn between anger at "their" men for falling victim to the stereotype of preferring white women as sexual partners, and anger at white women for seducing and taking away black men. The formula could be reversed, depending on which sex and which race you talked about. But the overall result was a new level of awareness that gender, as well as race, was an issue in this movement, and that until the question of treating women as equals became an explicit commitment of the movement, at least some of its ideals would always fall short of realization.

That became the context for the first tentative explorations of the "woman question" within SNCC. Casey Hayden and Mary King wrote a position paper on the movement's attitude toward women.

Sexual relationships between blacks and whites posed the ultimate challenge to the "establishment." Such relationships symbolized both the sexual revolution and the struggle for racial equality.

Stokely Carmichael, a veteran of CORE and other civil rights organizations, became president of SNCC in 1964. He gave public articulation to the phrase "black power"— initially coined by Willie Ricks—and later, with the political scientist Charles Hamilton, published a book by that title.

Within SNCC, Hayden and King argued, women were frequently treated with condescension, as though they were tokens to be tolerated, not respected. "[The] assumption of male superiority [among SNCC men]," they wrote, "[is] as widespread and deep-rooted and as crippling to the woman as the assumptions of white supremacy are to the Negro." No matter how much they might do to make the movement happen, women were never allowed to exercise power. "This is no more a man's world than it is a white world," the paper concluded, and if SNCC men did not realize that, women would have to force them to change.

As an early statement of feminist principles, the Hayden-King position paper brilliantly seized upon the underlying similarity between the gender and race issues. Its logic and emotion were overwhelming. Yet it came at a time in SNCC's history when the movement itself was not prepared to alter its course sufficiently to make equal treatment of women a priority of the same order as equal rights for blacks. Many SNCC men felt that their record on the issue was already better than that of most in the society; many black SNCC women saw the argument as relevant in a larger sense, but more the product of white women's experience than of their own in this situation. After an all day discussion at a staff retreat, the majority sentiment was to put the question of gender equality aside.

Within a year the Black Power faction of the civil rights movement, led by Stokely Carmichael, had risen to prominence in SNCC. Integration was now seen as a plot by whites to retain control of the movement, and many blacks became determined to seize control of their own agenda and exclude whites. But the white women who had first raised the issue of sex discrimination within SNCC did not lose the voices they had found. Rather, they intensified their efforts to evolve a set of principles on which women could unite together for *their* movement in the same way that blacks had united for theirs.

In "Sex and Caste: A Kind of Memo," Hayden and King elaborated on the lessons they had learned. Women, like blacks, they claimed, were "caught up in a common law caste system." Both privately and publicly, they were treated as different and inferior. The only answer to such treatment, they concluded, was for women to organize collectively on their own behalf. "Perhaps we can start to talk to each other more openly than in the past," they wrote, "and create a community of support for each other so we can deal with our-selves and others with integrity and therefore keep working." Ironi-cally, what Hayden and King were talking about was the same kind of support and communication that had always been a critical part of women's lives—in Hilda Newberry's life with her backyard com-munity, in Laura Whiting's with her church group, in Barbara Harris's with her work and schoolmates. But now this was a call with an avowedly political purpose—to take the shared issues they and other women had talked about for years and make these the foundation for a collective act of rebellion.

The final ingredient for the rebirth of feminism took place within the rapidly expanding student movement in America. It would be historically inaccurate to speak of that movement as a unified cru-sade with a changing shape and definition. It took as many forms as there were issues, its ideological variants sufficient in number to fill a textbook. There were some who believed that a new culture, a "counterculture," offered the only way to change America, and oth-ers who embraced political revolution, even if it had to include vio-lence. Some wore overalls, T-shirts, and love beads and sought to transform the materialism of the middle class by creating a totally alternative life-style; others opted for factory jobs, short hair, and rimless glasses, committed to subverting the system from within.

Nevertheless, some generalizations are valid. Virtually all the participants in the student movement were white. Most came from middle- or upper-class backgrounds. Children of privilege, they shared something in common with the critical and reflective posture of the Fetter Family, the group of Protestant students in Boston seeking reform of the church. But they had gone far beyond the moderate optimism of that group, and even the more pointed skepticism of Students for a Democratic Society's (SDS) 1962 Port Huron state-ment, with its desire to humanize capitalism and technocracy. By the mid-1960s, when the student movement started to grow with explosive force, more and more young people began to question the very basis for their society. The Vietnam War radicalized youthful protestors, male and female alike, seeming to symbolize—with its use of napalm to burn down forests and search and destroy missions to annihilate the enemy—the dehumanizing aspects of capitalism and Western-style democracy.

One of the goals of Students for a Democratic Society (SDS) was to humanize the lot of the working person. But significantly, its leadership was primarily male, and the cover of this publication portrays male workers.

The 1969 Woodstock festival, advertised as "three days of peace and music and love," turned out to be a bit more chaotic when more than 300,000 young people showed up. Drug use, overcrowding, and poor sanitation—as well as an array of stars like Bob Dylan and Joan Baez— attracted worldwide media attention, and Woodstock became a symbol of the 1960s counterculture.

As student radicals set out in multiple ways to find a way of turning America around from its foreign policy in Vietnam, there were few constants that emerged from the tactics and philosophies of various protest groups. But two things at least could be said of those who seized the headlines: they became ever more militant in the tactics and ideas they entertained for challenging the establishment; and with virtually no exceptions, the men in the movements treated women as inferiors. "Macho" radicalism seemed the wave of the future—except that the women of the various movements would have none of it.

Some of the paternalism of the student movement reflected classic unconscious assumptions. "We regard *men* as infinitely precious and possessed of unfulfilled capacities for reason, freedom and love," the Port Huron statement had said—as if from the Declaration of

Students at the University of California at Berkeley demonstrate against the Vietnam War in 1967. Skills honed in the antiwar movement were later applied to the cause of women's and minority rights.

Independence in 1776 to the present day nothing had happened to alter the presumption that citizens were men. At other times, though, men in the movement seemed to intentionally regard women as inferior. At one SDS convention, an observer noted, "Women made peanut butter, waited on table, cleaned up, [and] got laid. That was their role." Todd Gitlin, president of SDS in the mid-1960s, noted that the whole movement was characterized by "arrogance, elitism, competitiveness, . . . ruthlessness, guilt—replication of patterns of domination . . . [that] we have been taught since the cradle." Women might staff inner-city welfare projects and immerse themselves, far more than men, in the life of the particular community being organized, but when it came to respect and recognition, they ceased being visible. Women occupied only 6 percent of SDS's executive committee seats in 1964.

Nor was SDS alone in its attitudes. Throughout the entire antiwar movement, a similar condescension and disregard prevailed, symbolized by the antiwar slogan, "Girls say yes to guys [not boys] who say no." Always happy to accept the part of the sexual revolution that allegedly made women more ready to share their affection, male radicals displayed no comparable willingness to share their own authority as part of a larger revolution. Women's equality was not part of the new politics any more than it had been part of the old.

The peace symbol was ubiquitous on clothing and printed materials as American public opinion turned increasingly hostile to the nation's involvement in Vietnam.

No event better symbolized the underlying antifeminist sentiment of the New Left than a demonstration against the war that took place in Washington, D.C., in 1969. Women were an integral part of the larger coalition of groups running the antiwar rally, but they felt as though some of their concerns as women should be addressed as well. The men resisted but finally agreed that, toward the end of the program, a woman representing these concerns would be allowed to speak. As soon as she took the microphone, men in the audience started to hoot her down.

In the face of such treatment, women members of the student

Women relied on their traditional role as peacemakers—a role they had also played in both world wars—in the movement to end the war in Vietnam.

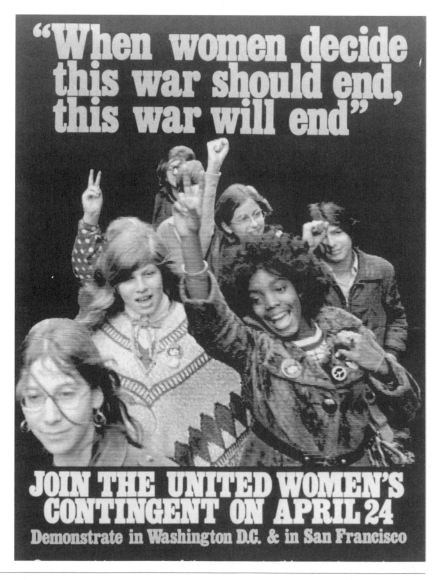

"When women decide this war should end, this war will end"

JOIN THE UNITED WOMEN'S CONTINGENT ON APRIL 24
Demonstrate in Washington D.C. & in San Francisco

movement began to arrive at the same conclusions reached by Casey Hayden and Mary King in "A Kind of Memo." But the women of the New Left never had the positive experience of the "beloved community" that veterans of the civil rights movement had shared. Consequently, their anger was greater, their radicalism more pointed. The process of finding a collective voice was the same. After a workshop in which women activists expressed their grievances, one participant wrote, "for many . . . it was the first [experience] of caring for other women—the feeling that women should organize women and [that] situations had to be developed so women could support other women." Moving beyond where Hayden and King left off, the women of the student movement had learned from bitter experience that they had to seize their own agenda, organize as separatist groups excluding men, and develop a program for change that dealt exclusively with the interests of women as women.

As the women's liberation movement spread from campus to campus and city to city, so too did consciousness-raising groups, the new instrument for mobilizing, then institutionalizing, a sense of collective self. If male values and organizations were the source of the problem with the larger society, women would have to create their own institutions, their own values, and their own way of making decisions and relating to each other. It was through this intimate process of self-disclosure and self-discovery that women's liberation quickly developed its most famous insight: that the personal is political. As church-activist-turned-radical-feminist Charlotte Bunch declared: "there is no private domain of a person's life that is not political and there is no political issue that is not ultimately personal."

The women in these groups came to understand that the pain and dissatisfaction of their own personal relationships with men was not something they were responsible for but rather reflected the whole system of hierarchy and power that existed "out there" in a male-dominated system designed to oppress women. Therefore, if women were to turn the world upside down, they had to begin by creating true democracy in their relationships with each other, then carry those values and ways of making decisions into the public arena and transform it as well. That way, the solution, as well as the cause of the problem, would link the personal and the political.

None of this, they decided, could happen through traditional

Charlotte Bunch, an activist brought up in the Methodist church, became a leader of the women's liberation movement and subsequently became associated with the Furies, a lesbian feminist group in Washington, D.C.

institutions with their hierarchies and male values. Rather, women had to occupy their own social space, develop their own definition of who they were, and their own agenda for where they wished to go. In an age when radicalism had become almost a cliché, this was perhaps the most revolutionary idea of all—taking control of their own lives and refusing to be subservient to what someone else said was their "proper place."

By the end of the 1960s, therefore, the foundation had been created for a widespread assault on traditional attitudes and values regarding sex roles in America. The issues could not be summarized easily or quickly. They involved not just questions of equal pay and the chance to compete one on one with men for a law partnership or medical residency. Rather, they were inclusive and varied in nature, ranging from abolishing sexist language like "chick" or "girl" to preserving and protecting woman's reproductive freedom of choice, eliminating sexist stereotypes from children's books, and defending a person's sexual orientation. Some women chose to organize feminist political caucuses, others created committees on the status of women in all the professions, and still others organized a woman's legal defense fund to fight in court on behalf of women's rights. Countless women joined the battle to heighten public consciousness about rape and domestic violence against women.

Precisely because the issues were so varied, they affected thousands of different groups and virtually every aspect of American life. For the same reason, however, this was no monolithic movement with a single director, program, or credo. The good part of that was that a group of women could enter into the movement in many places and feel comfortable. The bad part was that at times energies seemed divided, and disagreement rather than consensus prevailed over what needed to be done first, or next.

The key issue was how the broad expanse of American women (and men) would receive these multiple messages. Because women were part of every class, religion, and ethnic subgroup in America, the variation in the messages of the women's movements would presumably enhance the chances that different groups of women would respond positively to one or another of the issues being raised. On the other hand, the extent to which the various women's movements seemed to ignore or condescend in their own way to those not yet

One of the main goals of the women's movement was equal opportunity for working women. Here, pickets outside the Oberlin (Ohio) Telephone Company lobby for women's advancement in an industry in which women had tradition-ally been limited to jobs as operators.

"enlightened" could set in motion a powerful backlash. In geological terms, the women of NOW, the civil rights struggle, and the student movement had created the basis for a seismic shift in the political and cultural landscape of America. Whether it would become an earth-quake or just a tremor depended on how people responded.

CHAPTER 4

WHICH ROAD TO TRAVEL

Ultimately, the words used to describe how much change occurred in gender relationships after the 1960s would depend on the standard of measurement being used. If a woman defined equality as having her husband share responsibility for feeding and diapering a baby, then drawing up a schedule for allocating such tasks on a weekly basis could easily qualify as an earthquake. On the other hand, if equality were conceived as an end to institutions that were male-dominated and that were shaped by "masculine" values of competition and winning, then a shift in how one household organized its division of labor would seem fairly trivial. Part of the problem the new women's movement faced was that people started from different places and had different goals. Moreover, those goals could change over time: the same woman who in December 1968 believed greater help from her husband might constitute a revolution could easily conclude a year later that marriage itself was the source of all oppression and that reform of existing institutions was just a trick to perpetuate the status quo.

One way to trace the options available to women activists at the end of the 1960s is to look at the differences in philosophy and tactics that distinguished various feminist groups from each other,

A 1975 demonstration for the Equal Rights Amendment in New York City brought together a coalition of groups, including NOW, the YMCA, and labor unions. Behind the speaker, city councilwoman Miriam Friedlander, is council president Paul O'Dwyer; holding the Elected Black Democrats sign is David Dinkins, who would later become the first black mayor of New York City.

then to follow several individuals as they chose the path appropriate for them.

From the time the women's rights movement started in the United States in the 1840s, there was always a division between those who believed fundamentally that women were *individuals* and should be treated exactly the same as men and those who believed women were different, biologically and psychologically, and should be allowed to act *collectively* to implement their distinctive mission. The division of opinion could be seen clearly in the arguments made for the 19th Amendment, which granted woman suffrage. Some said women should have the vote because it was their natural right as individual citizens to participate in the electoral process; others insisted that women needed the vote because they were, as settlement house leader Jane Addams said, the "housekeepers" of the nation. Just as the family needed men and women to fill complementary roles based on their sexual identity, so too the country required women to vote in order that they could fulfill their special task of overseeing the national family's moral and spiritual health. This distinction remained a philosophical touchstone that continued to shape divergent approaches to feminism's agenda.

Among other things, these arguments help explain the difference in goals and tactics between liberal feminism, with its focus on individual rights, and radical feminism, with its concern for group advancement and activities. When the liberal National Organization for Women (NOW) was formed in 1966, it became the premiere civil rights group fighting for individual advancement for women. NOW used court cases, lobbied with Congress, and pressured the President to lower barriers against women. One of NOW's central demands was enactment and ratification of the Equal Rights Amendment (ERA)—a measure that would abolish sex as a category for treating women and men differently under the law. The ERA represented a quintessentially individualist approach to equality: its goal was a society in which women and men had identical status as individual human beings.

Implicit in this approach was a willingness to accept as basically sound the existing structure of the society, including the values underlying social and economic institutions. The goal was to secure women's acceptance as individuals within these institutions on the

The title of this pamphlet, published by NOW, is a play on the movie I Am Curious—Yellow.

In the 1960s, it was customary for classified ads to be separated into "Help, Women" and "Help, Men." The eye-catching headline "Girls Girls Girls" in the left column was a typical come-on for the clerical positions reserved for women.

In 1967 the board of the U.S. Steel Corporation, like that of most American corporations, was entirely male. Over the next 25 years, more and more women were added to these boards, but in many instances, they were appointed as "tokens" rather than in proportion to their numbers in the population or even in the managerial ranks.

principle of equal opportunity. Women should be granted the same opportunity to become chief executives and board members of corporations as men had. Therefore, NOW concentrated on destroying any obstacle that defined women as different in rights or abilities from men. NOW forced the *New York Times,* for example, to abolish classified ads that specified "Male Only" or "Female Only" jobs. It also integrated a series of bars and restaurants that in the past had excluded women. But at no time did NOW question corporate domination of American culture or the existing two-party political system. It sought instead to have women enter into these arrangements on the same basis as men. Integration, not separation, was its goal; reform, not revolution.

Radical feminists, by contrast, emphasized the need to turn society upside down by acting collectively to attack the roots of women's oppression. In the beginning the "radical" part of radical feminism reflected an attachment to the student Left of the late 1960s; but by the early 1970s, it spoke more to the determination of radical feminists to cut to the heart of the problem. For most women who called themselves radical feminists, the problem was the system of patriarchy—those social, economic, and cultural institutions that supported male supremacy. As long as women were trained by patriarchal institutions such as schools and churches to defer to men and suppress their own desires, they could not be free.

According to this analysis, women constituted an oppressed political "class." Their oppressor, in turn, was "the class of men, or the male role," as one radical feminist put it. As in any system of subordination, one class remained in control of the other by dividing and conquering its victims, or even worse, persuading its victims that they deserved to be subordinate. "The key to maintaining the oppressor role," New York feminist Ti-Grace Atkinson wrote, "is to prevent the oppressed from uniting." In a patriarchy men did this to women by socializing them to believe in "love," using romantic relationships to co-opt women into accepting their own oppression, and creating such institutions as marriage and the family to reinforce their bondage. Other institutions in the society—corporations, schools, churches, and government—simply replicated this class relationship, creating the equivalent of a closed system in which women, the majority of the world's population, were fooled into accepting an inferior and powerless role.

The response to such class subjugation was clear: women had to unite to throw off their oppression. "We need not only separate groups, but a separate movement," one radical feminist wrote. Coalition with men was a cultural and political contradiction, since it would lead only to a new version of women's subservience and defeat. Rather, women had to fight for themselves. As a class, women had different values and concerns than men had. What they needed was not acceptance as individuals into patriarchal institutions, but the kind of class solidarity as women that would permit their distinctive values to flower and triumph. If male-dominated institutions and values were the problem, women must then develop their own institutions—reflecting their own values—and make these the cornerstone for women's independence.

Radical feminists thus devoted much of their energy to building woman-defined and woman-run structures. Sometimes these were cultural, such as publishing houses, journals, and newsletters. At other times they were health-related—separate women-run clinics, for example, or centers for women seeking abortions or needing counseling or assistance in the face of domestic abuse from men.

Lesbian feminists participated in all forms of the women's liberation movement, but there also developed during the 1970s a much clearer sense among some lesbians of the need for a separate move-

Ti-Grace Atkinson, a former president of the New York chapter of the National Organization for Women, founded the Feminists in 1968, an early radical feminist group.

At the Valley Women's Center in Northampton, Massachusetts, women organized to work on causes such as abortion rights and racial matters (a sign on the wall advocates the cause of black radical Angela Davis) and also provided child care.

ment devoted to lesbian issues and concerns. By their commitment to other women as well as their rejection of sexual ties with men, lesbian feminists demonstrated their own determination to be independent of patriarchal controls. Moreover, in their emerging consciousness of the need to affirm their own identity as distinctive from heterosexual feminists, lesbian feminists were claiming a voice and a collective sense of self that significantly broadened and deepened the range of feminist constituencies.

Whatever the importance of these internal differences, most radical feminists were nevertheless more similar to each other than to liberal feminists. They might eventually want to be equal with men as individuals, but they sought first to be independent from men and to celebrate their collective identity as a class, nourishing those values and attitudes that emphasized their differences rather than their similarity to men.

Adopting a similar antiliberal approach, socialist-feminists also focused on the need for revolution rather than reform. Only for them, the class to be overthrown was capitalism, not men, and the means to secure that end was by uniting with all other oppressed groups of the world. Socialist-feminists also believed in solidarity, but they did not support separatism among women. They would continue to protest against the sexism displayed by men who were oppressed, but they would do so in the context of recognizing that the ultimate source of women's inequality was not men but rather the power of a

At the National March on Washington for Lesbian and Gay Rights in October 1979, homosexuals took their cause to the Capitol. Lesbian concerns took an increasingly prominent place in the women's movement.

capitalist class that included women as well as men. The fact that top executives at General Motors might include women did not make GM any less exploitative. "Women's liberation does not mean equality with men," one writer observed, "[because] equality in an unjust society is meaningless."

From the perspective of socialist feminists, the program of NOW could easily be implemented without changing a single power reality. "The establishment will have no problem whatsoever in assimilating [liberal feminists] by meeting their basic demands," Marlene Dixon, a socialist-feminist wrote. "In the future we can expect limited and elitist day-care programs, . . . abortion repeal; an effective end to job discrimination at least on the elite level. . . . All of these programs give the illusion of success while in fact assuring the destruction of any hope for women's liberation." Only when the fundamental institutions of society were overhauled would true equality become attainable.

Clearly, socialist feminists were very different from radical feminists in their assessment of where the roots of oppression lay and how best to mobilize to secure freedom. Yet both approaches shared a commitment to a collectivist rather than an individualist program of change. And both also saw the source of women's inequality as structural and fundamental and therefore solvable through reform. Whatever their own respective conflicts over who constituted a class and what revolution would mean, radicals and socialists seemed to

For women who returned to paid employment after the birth of their children, child care was a matter of great concern. Indeed, many women found their own employment caring for the children of other working women.

embrace a vision worlds apart from that of the women who started NOW and emerged from the networks of women reformers put in place by the state commissions on the status of women. How, then, could they be conceived as part of the same movement? And what would individual women do when confronted by such definitions of what feminism was all about? Above all, how would average women perceive and respond to such a bewildering array of pronouncements?

The truth was it was very difficult for women beyond a certain age to identify with either radical or socialist feminism. Laura Whiting or Hilda Newberry might decide that the ERA made sense as a long overdue recognition of women's right to legal equality; they would probably support the Equal Pay Act; and they might even imagine themselves as participants in and victims of Betty Friedan's "feminine mystique," sharing with Friedan's characters a "problem that has no name." After all, when Laura Whiting's husband forbade her to work, had he not been denying her the right to an identity of her own? And was not Hilda Newberry's life in the suburbs somewhat similar to what Friedan described, especially life in its more claustrophobic moments? Perhaps both women were conscious of having encountered the patriarchy—though they never would have called it that. Still, the furthest either of them would have been likely to go was to entertain some positive feeling about the ideas that NOW put forward in the late 1960s.

On the other hand, their daughters might easily have listened more readily to all three approaches to women's situation. Social surveys showed that daughters of women who had taken jobs in the aftermath of World War II were more likely to see themselves as playing a variety of roles in the world and as having a definition of marriage and family in which the husband and wife were equal partners. These same young women—and their brothers—had lived through the civil rights struggle—a struggle that generated expanding sensitivity about social inequality. At a time when the possibilities for social change were exploding at an unprecedented rate, it was likely that a younger generation would feel more comfortable in exploring all the ideas that emerged from the feminist movement.

Despite the differences between various feminist approaches, there was more overlap than one might think. Radical feminists took the lead in protesting the Miss America contest in Atlantic City as a "meat market." But it was not just radicals who recognized the exploitation involved in such a cultural ritual or the ruthlessness of the female fashion and cosmetics tycoons who promoted the products that ensnared women in this sexual captivity.

Furthermore, all women activists, whatever their organizational affiliation, could easily support abortion reform, the ERA, or the campaign for better day care. One did not have to believe a particular program represented a cure-all to see it as a step in the right direction. And perhaps for that reason people found it possible to move in and out of a variety of feminist groups in their quest for the road they most wished to travel.

Jane McCall graduated from college in 1963, the year that Betty Friedan's *The Feminine Mystique* was published. The daughter of a woman who had once aspired to become a doctor, Jane took her own ideas seriously. Although she had conformed to the gender expectations of the 1950s and participated in traditional middle-class female cliques while in high school, she was inspired by the social change movements of the early 1960s and came to question the structures of the society in which she had grown up.

In college, Jane had read Simone de Beauvoir's *The Second Sex*—a book that brilliantly describes how women are always treated by men as objects. It also describes how men project onto women char-

key
to
a
new
car:

A Union Trust Low-Cost Auto Loan

Take up to three years to repay. Insurance included
if desired. Action same day. Low bank rates.
Phone EXecutive 3-4400 or visit

UNION TRUST COMPANY

of the District of Columbia

Every Banking Service • Member Federal Deposit Insurance Corporation

Fourteenth Street Branch: Munsey Branch: Wisconsin and Western Branch:
FOURTEENTH STREET AT G, N.W.   1329 E STREET, N.W.   5351 WISCONSIN AVENUE, N.W.

In this 1960 advertisement there is no doubt who holds the power. The women's movement sought to eliminate such obviously skewed relationships between men and women.

acteristics and emotions they choose not to recognize in themselves but which they can now stereotype as "feminine." Now, reading Friedan, Jane became confirmed in her interest in feminist issues. She was especially struck by the way women's roles were confined to the home. Although in college she planned to set aside a minimum of two years to care for each of her children (she planned on having four), she was also determined to reenter the work world. She was not ready to buy into the world Friedan had portrayed, where advertisers and social scientists persuaded women to be happy with a lifetime of subservience. Friedan and de Beauvoir had helped to create for Jane a new set of lenses through which she observed her own life and that of the society around her.

Those lenses became more sharply focused when the women's liberation movement entered Jane's life. The movement took root everywhere, but especially in large cities and around college campuses. With a young child, Jane moved with her husband to a small college where she heard about a consciousness-raising group that had just started. She joined immediately. Some of the other women were also married and had children. Others were single.

A radical feminist had started the group and introduced ideas and readings that galvanized discussion. The "cr" group became a life-changing experience. The women developed a community of support and revelation as each week they explored their individual and collective experiences of growing up female in America. The topics were endless: "playing dumb" on dates, discovering their own sexuality, inequality in the roles of husbands and wives, snide jokes from comedians, and derisive comments by men on the street.

Sometimes the discussion turned to lesbianism and whether that

This cartoon illustrated a feminist newsletter describing the benefits of consciousness-raising groups. "Consciousness-raising (c-r)," it said, "is the very foundation of the Feminist Movement."

might not be a better, more rewarding kind of relationship. One or two of the women confessed to their own experiences with homosexuality and their desire to explore that possibility further. At other times the women focused on the complete inequality that characterized their home lives, with men simply assuming they would be waited on, and women expected to do all the cleaning, child care, and shopping.

It was an experience of another world—a "woman-defined" world. Jane shared with her husband only some of the insights she derived from the group meetings because the women had taken vows of confidentiality. But the discussions provided her with the support and reinforcement she needed to demand changes at home. One day she compiled a list that showed how many hours she spent on the work of the home and how many hours her husband spent. The ratio was 80 to 15. She demanded that changes be made, and reluctantly he agreed, sensing that a sea change was taking place in her life and that he might be washed ashore if he did not respond.

When Jane and her husband moved to a different university, she continued her involvement in the women's movement—and also her effort to build an egalitarian marriage and raise "her" children. For more than a year she helped lead a consciousness-raising collective, which had as its mission starting a whole series of "cr" groups that

A group called Lollipop Power published Martin's Father *along with many other nonsexist children's books as part of a collective publishing effort in the American South.*

could expand and spread the feminist message of self-organizing. Then she joined a publishing collective that specialized in writing and distributing children's books that avoided sexist stereotypes. One of these books was called *Martin's Father* and emphasized the warm and nurturing relationships a child could have with a male parent. Others portrayed girls as independent, assertive, and competent. Because Jane was a teacher, the children's books addressed a need she saw in her professional life as well as in her creative and political life.

Eventually, Jane moved on to make abortion rights her primary political activity. Again there was a direct connection to her professional life because she had pursued graduate training in social work and was now an abortion counselor. A different, much more classically "political" task, organizing for abortion rights meant building coalitions, lobbying the state legislature, and closely allying with groups like the National Abortion Rights Action League (NARAL) and NOW. In a period of six years Jane had moved in her own experience from focusing on "cr" groups to participating in a "separatist" publishing venture to joining an organization that most would have seen as mainstream politics.

If one chose to use categories of feminist activity, one could say that Jane had proceeded from a "radical-feminist" starting point to the legislative focus of liberal feminism. Yet she did not see those categories as either relevant or meaningful. At each stage of her involvement she had worked with some women who were lesbian feminists and believed strongly in separatism, but also with "straight" women who saw their feminist work as consistent with remaining in a marriage relationship. There were so many different things to do that there was no point in devoting excessive time to thinking about labels. Jane had simply followed her own interests in women's issues wherever they led her. In the process she explored many of the roads available within the feminist movement.

Celeste Bagley went through a process similar to Jane's but with a slightly different outcome. The daughter of a Methodist minister, she had been involved in civil rights activities throughout the mid-1960s in the Southern city where she went to college. As a direct outgrowth of participating in that movement, she became interested in the emerging women's liberation struggle. She had participated

The National Organization for Women sponsored this demonstration outside the White House in 1969. Some women were tethered by symbolic chains.

in a variety of New Left activities and had witnessed firsthand the crude machismo tactics of some of the male radicals. Consequently, when she moved to a northern city, she became one of the founders of a radical feminist group that began with consciousness-raising but extended to support of other separatist activities as well. Her group helped initiate demonstrations similar to the Miss America protests in Atlantic City in 1968.

When Celeste moved to another university town, she too became involved in creating the publishing collective that focused on nonsexist children's books. There she eventually met Jane. At the same time, Celeste was organizing women at the university to protest the absence of women faculty members and the male bias of the curriculum. From her civil rights days forward, however, Celeste had been at heart a movement person, and for her the core of the civil rights and New Left movements had been their commitment to fundamental change in the social and economic order. That was a commitment Celeste wanted to maintain in her feminist politics as well.

Consequently, Celeste became one of the founding members of a socialist feminist collective. Through her involvement in this new collective, Celeste and her sister feminists sought to sustain a focus on issues of economic inequality. She was especially concerned with the insidious ways that working women who were hospital attendants or domestic servants were treated like dirt by their employers. It was important, she believed, for women doctors to align themselves with women orderlies who were underpaid and overworked. Trying to forge cross-class and cross-racial alliances, the new collective was willing to entertain coalition with other "left" groups, however bad their "macho" pasts, in order to attack the economic system that was the primary villain in women's lives. Persisting in her overall concern with the larger framework of social and economic justice for all, Celeste eventually took a position at a large university and carried her concerns into her work developing women's studies programs.

Elizabeth Appleby also had at least fleeting contact with Jane and Celeste. Somewhat younger than the other two, she attended college in the late 1960s and early 1970s, when the women's liberation movement was already a strong presence on most campuses. Elizabeth joined some of the women's liberation groups at her university, seeking the combination of people and concerns most consistent with her own interests. Elizabeth was a lesbian and knew that commitment to gay rights was a prerequisite for whichever group

Women gradually made inroads into the corporate world, but as this cartoon demonstrates, it was difficult for them to escape men's traditional notions of their proper roles.

The newsletter of the radical organization Off Our Backs portrayed in graphic terms the new roles that women were taking on even as they continued to raise children. Expressing the disaffection of many women fed up with American culture, Off Our Backs served as a vehicle for alienated women to communicate with each other about their concerns and potential solutions to their oppression.

she joined. But she also knew that lesbians were ordinarily involved in most feminist groups and that there was a case to be made for working jointly with heterosexual women on a whole variety of issues as long as gay rights were not ignored. Thus, even as she joined the local gay and lesbian alliance, Elizabeth also participated in the feminist collective that published children's books and volunteered at the local rape-crisis center. Finally, she helped found a feminist newsletter that became a critical link in joining the various women's liberation groups throughout the region.

Also a collective, the newsletter sought to provide the network of communication by which women involved in the nearly endless

SUMMER DANCE

2nd ANNUAL BENEFIT FOR THE
UNION OF SEXUAL MINORITIES

Beer, Prizes   Earth Station 7   August 28
& Refreshments   402 15 Ave.   Saturday night at 8

                      donation requested   for childcare or
                                              information call
Labor donated 8/76   329-5186 or 324-5016

Lesbians increasingly found that they needed organizations separate from the women's movement to deal with issues related specifically to the gay community. This poster promotes a fund-raising dance for an organization founded in 1975.

feminist activities around the area could learn about each other and find ways of working together. Such newsletters had sprung up throughout the country. Sent to sister publications as part of a mutual exchange, these journals and letters became almost an invisible network tying feminists to each other, offering ideas, reinforcement, and encouragement. Most of the members of the collective Elizabeth worked with were lesbians, but "straight" women participated as well. The newsletter sought to publicize the full range of feminist activities going on in the area, from NOW meetings, to demonstrations on behalf of abortion rights, to gatherings on behalf of gay and lesbian rights.

Eventually, however, the members of the newsletter collective came to feel that gay and lesbian concerns were being ignored by too many of the women's groups in the area and that even where they were recognized they occupied a subordinate place. For too long, they felt, gay women had submerged their own concerns for the greater good of the feminist coalition. Hence the newsletter collective decided to make itself primarily a vehicle for promoting and advertising activities of concern to lesbian activists. Other feminist activities would still receive mention. But a lesbian perspective would now predominate.

Interestingly, each of these feminist activists ended up on a different road. An outside observer might look at where they ended up and conclude that they shared little in common. Jane McCall devoted most of her activity to concerns that would be called part of liberal feminism's agenda—working for equal rights under the law within the existing social system. Lobbying the state legislature to fund abortions for poor women was a lot different than trying to overthrow capitalism. Celeste Bagley, on the other hand, chose to focus on the broad collective agenda embodied in the vision of socialist feminism. She would seek a coalition of oppressed groups to work together to transform the social and economic system that was ultimately responsible for women's oppression. Finally, Elizabeth Appleby decided to devote herself to a separatist collective that defended the tenets of radical feminism, saw patriarchy and the "male class" as the primary source of oppression, and lesbian feminism as the best solution to that oppression.

An aptly named bottle of laundry detergent becomes the icon of a demonstrator at a 1978 rally for the Equal Rights Amendment in Washington, D.C.

Certainly in the larger culture these differences became a primary source of contention and division. Some socialist feminists dismissed groups like NOW as substitutes for the establishment that cared only about getting a few more women executives into the exploitative ruling class. Socialists also dismissed radical feminists as being too inward looking and unpolitical. Radical feminists, one socialist said, used celebrations of sisterhood as a basis for "isolating ourselves from issues not directly related to our status as women." Radical feminists, in turn, found it easy to dismiss both liberals and socialists as too male-centered, willing to accept coalition with the oppressor as a vehicle for progress when in fact they were simply perpetuating their own bondage. Liberal feminists, finally, perceived both radical and socialist feminists as indulging in romantic illu-

"Warhol...the ultimate voyeur...
foiled by S.C.U.M...." (Time)
"A diatribe of fanatical intensity...
savage shrewdness and wit." (Newsweek)

S.C.U.M.
Society for Cutting Up Men
MANIFESTO
by Valerie Solanas

with a Commentary by Paul Krassner

The crude language and radical tenets of organizations such as S.C.U.M. polarized the women's movement.

Joined by his three daughters, actor Alan Alda, a firm supporter of women's rights, speaks at an ERA rally in 1981. From left are Helen Milliken, Susan Ford Vance (daughter of former President Gerald Ford), and Eleanor Smeal, president of NOW.

sion. Betty Friedan denounced the "sexual shock-tactics and man-hating" of radical feminists, singling out for special contempt the "lavender menace" of lesbian feminists, whom she believed would alienate support for broader women's rights objectives. Similarly, liberal feminists rejected the rhetoric of socialist feminists as so much hot air. Liberals were working for real change while socialist feminists were spouting hothouse revolutionary slogans.

Yet, as the cases of Jane McCall, Celeste Bagley, and Elizabeth Appleby illustrate, real women in real places did not fall easily into such categories of ideological contention. Rather, they were as likely as not to have participated in a variety of different kinds of feminism, moving naturally and without great anxiety or stress from one to the other. To be sure, each ended up on a different road as the ultimate choice was made as to which path to follow. But usually this was a product of personal interests and evolving priorities. More often than not, the transitions evolved as part of a progression along a single journey, not a leap from one ideological fortress to another.

Arguably, the same emphasis on continuity was justified on the national scene as well. Certainly the divisions remained, and on occasion became highlighted when such prominent individuals as Betty Friedan or Ti-Grace Atkinson made pronouncements. Yet nationally as well, there was movement between approaches. Notwithstanding Friedan's concern over the "lavender menace," NOW created a task force on sexuality and lesbianism in the early 1970s and appeared to display a greater commitment to gay rights. Radical feminists and socialist feminists joined liberal feminists on a whole series of issues, from abortion rights to the ERA, child care, and spouse abuse. NOW even emulated its critics on the Left, announcing as its slogan for 1975, "Out of the Mainstream, Into the Revolution." To the average citizen there was more to unite feminists than to divide them.

The one glaring flaw that should have been of concern to all women activists, whatever their ideological persuasion, was the ongoing failure of feminism to escape its own narrow class and race boundaries. Despite the ambitious aspirations of socialist feminists for a cross-class, cross-race coalition, the fact remained that most feminist activists were white, middle class, and college-educated. There were occasional black feminist groups, such as the National Black Feminist Organization, and each feminist organization boasted some participation by African-American or Latina women. Yet on balance, the numbers were infinitesimally small. Both the language and the programs of feminist groups seemed to reflect a white middle-class approach. Until women of all classes and backgrounds felt both attracted to and welcomed by feminist groups, there would be little likelihood that the promise of a universal sisterhood could become a reality.

WHAT WERE THOSE WITCHES REALLY BREWING?

THE HIDDEN TAX ON BEING MARRIED

Ms.

SPECIAL SECTION: RUNNING FOR ANY OFFICE

AFTER THE MARRIAGE IS OVER — A DIARY

WHAT MOVIES HAVE DONE TO WOMEN

CHAPTER 5

RESPONSES

O ne measure of a social movement's success is the extent to which its ideas begin to affect people's behavior: how they talk, what they wear, what career choices they make, how they conduct themselves in the privacy of their bedrooms as well as on the job. Most social movements also seek to change public policy, hoping that transformations that occur in people's heads may be reflected in state regulations and programs as well.

By those criteria it seemed that feminism had registered a powerful impact on American society during the 1970s. It was not just that late-night comedians started to make jokes about women's liberation or that talk shows now considered sex equality a "hot" item. Women themselves changed their social and economic behavior, postponing marriage and childbearing and seeking new careers; at least some men became more aware of how language and etiquette reflected sexist assumptions; and politicians began to address issues of gender discrimination directly. By no means had nirvana been reached. When the manufacturer of Virginia Slims cigarettes decided to pitch its product specifically toward a female audience, it chose for its slogan "You've come a long way, Baby," suggesting a dual message—women's lives had changed, but women remained sex ob-

Ms. magazine was founded to address women's issues not covered by the traditional women's magazines.

A biology lab at Smith College, taught by Professor Lois Tewinkel. Women have traditionally been underrepresented in science and mathematics, and colleges have made particular efforts to expand the ranks of women scientists. Feminists paid particular attention to the problem of "math anxiety," a phenomenon experienced by elementary and high school students when confronted with the cultural expectation that boys were better than girls at math and science.

jects. Yet even though sexism was still rife, the evidence suggested that change remained the dominant theme of the day.

One sign of the shifts taking place appeared in a series of public opinion polls taken during the 1960s and 1970s. In 1962 George Gallup had found that two-thirds of all women were satisfied with their lives and did not desire major change. Eight years later—three to four years after the women's movement had started—the Roper polling organization posed the same general question. At that point, 50 percent of women wanted significant changes while 50 percent were satisfied. Four years after that, in 1974, the question was posed a third time. On this occasion the result was exactly the reverse of what it had been in 1962—two-thirds of women were dissatisfied and wanted to see significant change toward greater equality, while only one-third were content. The turnabout correlated directly with the emergence of an active feminist movement.

Even more impressive were the results among younger women, those most likely to have grown up with ideas about themselves that had been shaped by the new women's liberation movement. The pollster Daniel Yankelovich was stunned by the "wide and deep" acceptance of feminist ideas among the young. In two years the number of students who declared that women were an oppressed group had doubled; moreover, approximately 70 percent of women in college expressed agreement with the statement that "the idea that a woman's place is in the home is nonsense." It seemed that the generation that came of age in the years after Betty Friedan's *The Feminine Mys-*

tique was published had internalized a very different sense of who they were and what they should be doing than their mothers or grandmothers had.

These new attitudes seemed to translate quickly into behavior as well. Throughout the decades following the Great Depression, college-educated women had constituted a smaller proportion of doctors, lawyers, and other high-paying professions than they had in 1900. This was largely due to discrimination. Hospitals would not accept women interns, and law firms offered few partnerships to women. But it was also due to cultural attitudes transmitted by teachers and parents. Guidance counselors told female students that they should be nurses, not doctors, or that they should take classes to become secretaries rather than go to business schools to train as executives. As a result, from 1940 to 1970 the entering classes of medical, law, and business schools were only 5 percent to 8 percent female. As late as 1970, college men outnumbered women 8 to 1 in expressing interest in careers in engineering, medicine, and law.

By the mid-1970s, however, a sea change had occurred. The number of women planning to enter traditionally "feminine" careers, such as elementary school teaching or nursing, fell from 31 percent to 10 percent. In the meantime, women's applications to law and medical schools soared 500 percent, and by the mid-1980s, entering classes of medical, law, and business schools were 40 percent female. The percentage of new women doctors increased from 9 percent to 22 percent from 1971 to 1981, while the proportion of

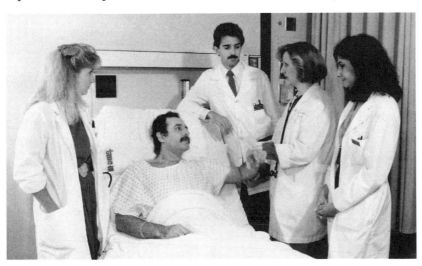

Dr. Sandra Willsie, a doctor at the University of Missouri, Kansas City, conducts rounds with both female and male medical students.

With the advent of the sexual revolution, organizations such as Planned Parenthood found an increasing need for their programs. Their services included birth control and counseling for sexually active couples.

women Ph.D.s leaped from 10 percent to 30 percent. Thirty years earlier, virtually all these women would have been entering "women's" jobs, with low prestige, limited chance for advancement, and poor pay. Now they were becoming increasingly competitive with men for high-paying, high-status jobs in the most prestigious professions. Once again the feminist movement seemed to have made a significant impact, supporting a very different idea of who a woman was, and what she could aspire to be, than had existed just a few years before.

Less related to feminism and perhaps more a consequence of the general "liberation" attitudes of the 1960s was a significant change in women's sexual behavior as well. There have really been two sexual revolutions in the 20th century. The first came in the early 1900s, when there was a significant increase in the number of women engaging in premarital intercourse and expressing satisfaction with their sexual experiences. Use of birth control also increased at that time. By the 1970s, however, that first revolution seemed mild. The number of women who believed that premarital sex was wrong fell from 75 percent in 1969 to 53 percent in 1974. Among younger women, especially, sexual behavior patterns became much more similar to those of men, with approximately 75 percent of women and men becoming sexually active by the age of 17.

The greatest indicator that feminism was now a significant presence in America appeared in the new, respectful attention that public policymakers paid to issues of gender. Largely in response to pressure from NOW, the Equal Employment Opportunity Commission (EEOC) began to devote as much time to complaints about gender discrimination as it had to grievances about racial discrimination. When it was discovered that 7 percent of all gender-related cases involved workers at American Telephone and Telegraph (AT&T), the commission filed a lawsuit on behalf of all women workers at that company. The result was a settlement involving back pay to women workers who had been denied equal treatment and a powerful affirmative action program to attract women employees. (Affirmative action programs provide limited kinds of preferential treatment, such as increased job opportunities and promotions, for members of groups that have historically been victims of long-term racial or gender-based discrimination.) AT&T started to desegregate its work

This photograph of a women "linesman" became an icon of the women's movement's success in finding work for women in jobs previously reserved for men.

force, with women taking positions repairing telephone lines (traditionally an all-male job) and men being hired as operators. The U.S. secretary of labor, in the meantime, announced in 1970 that from that point forward federal contracts would require the employment of a certain percentage of women.

Congress did its part by enacting a whole series of bills designed to end discrimination against women. It also provided support to programs of special interest to women. Title IX of the 1972 Educational Amendments Act prohibited any college or university that received federal aid from discriminating against women. Among other things, Title IX required that college athletic programs allocate scholarships to women athletes on the same basis as to men athletes. Congress also used the tax codes to provide benefits for young families using child care.

Title XI of the 1972 Educational Amendments Act required college sports to be funded equally for male and female students. Women's sports activities experienced tremendous growth as a result.

Most impressive was the move in Congress to pass the Equal Rights Amendment (ERA) and send it to the states for ratification. For 50 years the National Woman's Party had been seeking such action. For most of that period the ERA failed because other women's groups opposed it, believing that the amendment would nullify all special legislation designed to protect women's interests. By the 1960s, however, most women's groups had endorsed the ERA, and Congress responded. The ERA passed the House by a margin of 354 to 23, the Senate by 84 to 8. The action seemed to suggest that a feminist wave was sweeping the entire country.

In politics as well, women seemed to be making a major surge forward. A new National Women's Political Caucus was formed, representing elected officials as well as policymakers, to lobby for female representation in all government agencies as well as to support legislation of special interest to women. Individual members of Congress—such as Shirley Chisholm (the first black woman in Congress and a Presidential candidate in 1972), Bella Abzug (a prominent peace activist), and Sissy Farenthold (a Texas politician whose name was placed in nomination for Vice President on the 1972 Democratic ticket)—headlined the growing prominence of women as a political force. The number of women candidates for state legislative positions increased by 300 percent from 1972 to 1974; women's participation in party political conventions skyrocketed (from 13 percent in 1968 to 40 percent in 1972 among Democrats and from 17 percent to 30 percent among Republicans); and party leaders appeared to be embarked on a national competition to see which group could do more to attract women followers.

The federal court system also seemed responsive to the new feminist wave. Pauli Murray, a black lawyer (and subsequently one of the first black women to become an Episcopal priest), had pioneered the strategy of winning legal battles for women by using the equal protection clause of the 14th Amendment, which guaranteed every citizen equal treatment under the Constitution. Using this argument, Murray and a series of other women lawyers persuaded the courts that women could not be excluded from juries, that they had the same legal standing as men in being able to administer estates and handle property, and that they should be accorded the same status in relation to their dependents as men had always had.

Perhaps the most far-reaching court decision affecting women's lives was the Supreme Court case *Roe* v. *Wade* (1973). Jane Roe, a fictitious name for a young, single woman who was pregnant, sued on behalf of all other women for the right to have an abortion. Her lawyers argued that anti-abortion statutes violated women's right to privacy. They also contended that the right to privacy was guaranteed, implicitly, by the Bill of Rights of the Constitution. By a 7-to-2 vote the Supreme Court upheld their argument, viewing reproductive freedom as a fundamental right. In the specific case the Court ruled that women could have a medically safe abortion until the

In 1972 Shirley Chisholm, the first black woman in Congress, announced her candidacy for President.

Roe *v.* Wade *was a test case for the movement to keep abortion legal. Pro-choice advocates feared that if abortion were made illegal, poor women would have to return to dangerous and unsafe "back-room" abortionists.*

third trimester of a pregnancy. Women who had been forced to flee the country or resort to back-alley abortionists in order to terminate an unwanted pregnancy now had won the battle to exercise control over their bodies legally and openly.

Even institutions of popular culture reflected the changes. There had always been women's magazines—the *Ladies' Home Journal, McCall's,* and *Redbook,* to name just a few. But for the most part these journals reinforced traditional views of women's place in the social order. Advice columns provided counsel on how to keep a husband happy or deal with a problem child; recipe pages offered scores of new ideas on how to satisfy the family palate; and advertisements focused on selling products designed to enhance "femininity" or assist women in carrying out their ordained social roles as homemakers and mothers. These magazines certainly were not on the cutting edge of feminism.

But then in 1972 all that changed. Women journalists had already started to challenge the sexist assumptions of traditional journals, holding a sit-in at *Ladies' Home Journal* and suing *Time* and *Newsweek* for not recognizing adequately women's issues and their professional status as reporters. Now a group of women led by Gloria Steinem started to publish a different kind of woman's magazine. Entitled *Ms.,* the new journal explicitly identified itself as a voice of the woman's movement, committed in both its feature stories and its

The staff of Ms. *magazine meets with editor in chief Gloria Steinem (with long hair, center). The magazine advised that "men who really want to be helpful" with consciousness raising would "care for houses and children" so that women could attend their meetings.*

advertising to reinforce the tenets of feminism. Steinem had been a brilliant reporter who frequently found herself the victim of discrimination aimed at women. Because of the absence of abortion rights laws in America, she had been forced to have an illegal abortion. Often she had to write about "women's" topics from a traditional perspective in order to sell her stories. Once she had even posed as a *Playboy* bunny in order to write a piece for *Show* magazine.

But increasingly Steinem had been able to focus on political stories about civil rights and other burning social issues, which brought her into the feminist movement. When *Ms.* was first published, as a supplement to *New York Magazine,* it sold a quarter of a million copies. Soon it was on its own, galvanizing women readers with its array of successful writers—such as Alice Walker, Catharine Stimpson, and Letty Cotton Pogrebin—and its systematic evocation of the dynamic changes occurring daily in women's lives.

Ms. was particularly effective in the way it recognized and endorsed women's gradual yet startling realization of their own condition of inequality. The letters columns were full of stories describing the "click" that suddenly made a woman realize she was a victim, playing a part assigned to her by someone else, and thus denied her own voice and autonomy. It might come in the middle of the night when a woman's husband woke her saying, "The baby's crying, honey, you'd better see what's wrong" or when a young man persisted in

Several of the stories in the children's book Free to Be...You and Me *originally appeared in a special section of* Ms. *magazine. The book included poems such as "Don't Dress Your Cat in an Apron" and stories in which girls pitch on a softball team, princesses beat princes in footraces, and daddies cry.*

making romantic advances after the woman said to stop. But the "click" was there in a thousand manifestations that, through the medium of *Ms.*, now became the common property of women throughout the land. Not only was it okay to be a feminist, but it was a fact of life and a truth that readers could not imagine having missed for so long. *Ms.* became one of the staples of many women's lives, just as *McCall's* once had been. Only now the message was very different.

Even Hollywood stars became involved in promoting a different vision of how boys and girls should grow up. Led by actress Marlo Thomas, a group of entertainers concerned about how children were socialized into traditional roles of passivity (female) or aggression (male) by most fairy tales and children's books decided to celebrate diversity and autonomy. A record album, "Free To Be You and Me," was a series of songs, by stars everyone recognized, that told boys and girls it was all right for them to be whomever they wanted to be. Crying was something good for both boys and girls to do. Participating in sports, playing with dolls, and dressing up were also good. Dr. Benjamin Spock, the pediatrician who wrote the nation's leading advice book on how to raise children, even changed some of his counsel to young parents when he became aware that some of the old stereotypes of how to treat boys differently from girls were not only wrong but harmful.

Clearly, this new woman's movement was making a substantial impact. No matter where you looked—from the Supreme Court to the White House to the newsstand—women were being treated in a different fashion, demanding a different code of behavior, and translating into their daily lives a commitment to greater freedom than had ever been seen before in America. "I am woman, hear me roar," the entertainer Helen Reddy sang. "In numbers too large to ignore, . . . I am strong, I am invincible." There was a determination to reach an audience, to declare a message of independence, to seize a voice, and there were few who could avoid being aware that a cultural revolution was potentially on the way.

Yet all the visible evidence of change could not hide the fact that for most Americans, male and female, this was still just a news story. It might be interesting to talk about, but what did it mean? After all, women and men had to play different roles in society in order for things to work, didn't they? How could the family survive if women were not ultimately responsible for cooking the meals and raising the kids? And how could men retain their manhood if they were expected to do "women's work," such as cleaning the toilets and doing the laundry? Wasn't there something eternal about Adam and Eve and their differences that made all these feminist slogans more a passing fad than a deep-seated change?

Equally important, the other side had not yet been heard from. For the moment it seemed that all the energy and momentum were on the side of those supporting women's liberation. Whether it be *Ms.,* or TV star Mary Tyler Moore with her show about a career woman, or all the new women applicants to law school, it certainly looked as though the forces of change were in command. But there were also countless Americans who had not yet been heard from. Millions of women from ethnic and cultural minorities with a different set of traditions than "Anglo" women might not feel the same need to assert themselves as the women in NOW did. And millions more, perhaps, thought there was no reason to consider changing roles they believed to be divinely ordained.

Feminists might laugh scornfully at the advice columns in the *Ladies' Home Journal*, but countless others saw them as on target and much closer to what really counted than fantasies of independence. Thus the contest was not over. And if in 1973, with the ERA, *Roe* v. *Wade,* and *Ms.,* some feminists felt in command, it was far too soon to tell whether they had a reason to think that change was here to stay.

Dressed all in white, supporters of the Equal Rights Amendment bear the text of the proposed amendment through the streets of Washington, D.C., in 1977.

CHAPTER 6

THE COUNTERMOVEMENT

All during the 1960s, there had been developing in America a revulsion at what many citizens took to be the excesses of protest movements. For some it started with the transition within the civil rights movement from passive, nonviolent protest in pursuit of integration to the Black Power rhetoric ("Move on over Whitey, or we're gonna move on over you") of Stokely Carmichael. A world of difference seemed to separate Dr. King from the Black Panthers, who in 1968 marched with machine guns at their side into the California state legislature.

Still other Americans found their source of distress in the young college students with long hair, love beads, and scrawny jeans who hurled the epithet "pig" at police officers, denounced their country as corrupt and brutal, and then seized university offices and trashed their professors' files as a way of expressing disgust with the war in Vietnam. In 1968 and 1969 Columbia, Cornell, and Harvard were all held under siege at one time or another by student radicals. And as if that were not enough, there now appeared on the scene something called women's liberation. Feminists—at least some of them—celebrated homosexuality, denounced religion and the nuclear family as bastions of patriarchy, and saw salvation in a manless world where women could enshrine their own separate and superior values.

STOP-ERA leader Phyllis Schlafly addresses a rally in the Illinois State capitol in June 1978. The Illinois House of Representatives was scheduled to vote on the Equal Rights Amendment that week.

Not surprisingly, there was an overlap among people distressed by these views. The same people who felt their values and life-styles under attack from Black Power militants were likely to feel threatened by students or by "women's libbers." Social observers gave different names to this phenomenon. Some called those who were angry Middle Americans; others used the phrase the Silent Majority; by the mid-1970s, TV evangelist Jerry Falwell called his followers the Moral Majority. Whatever the name used, however, it usually described people who were working class or lower middle class in background and who had struggled all their lives to become part of the American Dream. They had toiled to buy a small house and perhaps send a child to college; they believed firmly in God and country; and now they saw all that they cherished in life being spit upon.

For many of these Middle Americans, feminism represented the epitome of what was wrong. After all, were traditional sex roles not the foundation of society? And if people stopped treating women like women, and men like men, everything would fall apart. From such a perspective, everything valuable in society—the family, the church, vows of fidelity, loyalty to country, love of parents—was based on men and women knowing their place and working together to make America great. Feminism, therefore, was about more than women's individual right to vote or have a career or manage their own institutions; above all, it was an attack on the very foundations of society. And that meant feminism must be opposed.

To women concerned with preserving the esteem and recognition conferred by traditional sex roles, the ERA encapsulated all that was dangerous in the feminist movement. If the ERA became law, they believed, all differences between the sexes would be abolished, and all institutions based on those differences would then self-destruct as well. The family was based on women and men performing complementary roles, with husbands and wives sharing a loyalty to the family that was more important than their individual lives. By contrast, the ERA seemed to these people to embody individualism run amok. Not only would men and women lose their distinctive identities: women would start placing their individual desires for fulfillment ahead of their obligation to the family. As one antifeminist wrote, "the humanist-feminist view of the family is that it is a biological, sociological unit in which the individual happens to reside; it has no meaning and purpose beyond that which each individual chooses to give it. . . .[In such a situation, the family] becomes an instrument of oppression and denial of individual rights."

Worst of all, from this point of view, was the degree to which feminism destroyed the softer, more nurturing and sacrificing side of women's nature and replaced it with the ideal of women acting like men. This "macho-feminism," as one person called it, "despises anything which seeks to interfere with the desires of Number One." Through such a selfish process, women's true nature was destroyed. "The less time women spend thinking about themselves," Connie Marshner, a leading antifeminist, wrote, "the happier they are . . . Women are ordained by nature to spend themselves in meeting the needs of others."

But if feminists had their way, selfishness would prevail over serving the family, and women would now compete with men for dominance and self-assertion rather than uniting with men for the greater good of the family unit. Whether the issue was abortion,

The Conservative Caucus Emergency Effort to STOP ERA

Dear Senator Hatch:

    I agree with you that if ERA is ever to be stopped, it is crucial that it be stopped in Florida, now!

    I want to do everything I can to help this urgent project of The Conservative Caucus - Stop ERA.

    I am enclosing my maximum contribution of $ _____ today, to help pay the costs of The Conservative Caucus Emergency Effort to Stop ERA in Florida -- and to help The Caucus meet its unpaid bills incurred in stopping ERA in North Carolina.

Sincerely,

Mr., Mrs., Miss _____

Address _____

City _____ State _____ Zip _____

A SPECIAL PROJECT OF THE CONSERVATIVE CAUCUS, INC. - STOP ERA
7777 LEESBURG PIKE, FALLS CHURCH, VIRGINIA 22043

[ ] Check here if you would like $5 of your contribution to pay for a subscription to TCC's Member's Report (4 issues per year).

Please make your check or money order payable to:
TCC PROJECT TO STOP ERA

A direct-mail fund-raising campaign was part of the effort by the Conservative Caucus to defeat the ERA. The return form gives contributors the choice of the titles Mr., Mrs., or Miss but not Ms.

careers, or questioning the value of lifetime loyalty to one's spouse, feminism seemed to want to elevate the self to a position of unquestioned supremacy. In the process, women—and men—would lose the family cohesion and loyalty that served as the model for everything else that was good about American civilization.

One of the first movements to counter feminism, therefore, focused on defeating the ERA. Led by Phyllis Schlafly, a conservative Republican with a master's degree in government from Radcliffe, the anti-ERA forces concentrated on mobilizing grass roots constituencies in each state to petition their state legislators not to ratify the ERA. The organizations had many names: STOP-ERA (STOP meant Stop Taking Our Privileges), WWWW (Women Who Want to be Women), and FLAG (Family, Liberty and God). But all had a common theme: defend the family and preserve the differences between the sexes. "God Almighty created men and women biologically different and with differing needs and roles," Jerry Falwell proclaimed. "Good husbands who are godly men are good leaders. Their wives and children want to follow them." According to Schlafly and her allies, if the ERA were successful, husbands would no longer be required to provide for wives; alimony (a divorced husband's responsibility to provide financially for his ex-wife) would cease; and protective labor laws that aided blue-collar women would be eliminated.

Most frightening of all, the God-ordained differences between men and women would be dissolved. In phrases reminiscent of the

Opponents of the ERA use catchy slogans to promote their cause on the steps of the U.S. Capitol.

The Phyllis Schlafly Report

VOL. 11, NO. 4, SECTION 2 BOX 618, ALTON, ILLINOIS 62002 NOVEMBER, 1977

Should the E.R.A. 7-Year Deadline Be Extended?

Memorandum on the Constitutionality of a Proposed Resolution to Extend the Time for Ratification of the Equal Rights Amendment Submitted to the U.S. House Subcommittee on Civil and Constitutional Rights of the Committee on the Judiciary, November 1977.

by Grover Rees, III

When the 92d Congress proposed the Equal Rights Amendment in 1972, the proposal [H.J. Res. 208] included a provision to the effect that the amendment would become part of the Constitution "when ratified by the legislatures of three-fourths of the several States within seven years from the date of its submission to the Congress[.]" That seven-year period will end in March, 1979. A resolution proposed in the 95th Congress would extend the period within which states may ratify.

The proposed resolution is clearly unconstitutional --- or, perhaps more accurately, could not constitutionally be given the effect apparently desired by its proponents. If it met the formal requisites for a resolution proposing a constitutional amendment, such a resolution *would* have the effect of beginning a new period wherein states could ratify the E.R.A.; but states which ratified under the 1972 resolution could not be presumed (or forced) to acquiesce in the "extension."

This conclusion --- that Congress cannot, as an incident to its power to propose an amendment, retrospectively change the conditions under which the states were led to believe they were ratifying --- proceeds inevitably from the principles underlying Article V of the Constitution. A careful analysis of the somewhat confused jurisprudence construing Article V would also tend to support such a result.

1) Principles of Construction of Article V.

Article Five should be construed in light of the Framers' understanding of the Constitution as a compact among the states. Whatever the remaining utility of the concept of "independent sovereigns" in other areas of constitutional law, it is simply impossible to understand the amending process without resort to such a doctrine. The three numbers of *The Federalist Papers* dealing with constitutional amendments all speak of a compact between "distinct and independent sovereigns" (No. 40, Madison), or in similar terms (e.g., until all thirteen colonies agree to the Constitution, "no political relations can subsist between the assenting and dissenting States," (No. 43, Madison); "[t]he compacts which are to embrace thirteen distinct States in a common bond of amity and union," (No. 85, Hamilton).

Thus, where Article V is silent, it is appropriate to apply contract law to analyze whether the *contemporaneous consent* of three-fourths of the states has been given to a proposed amendment. This is true not only because the Framers expected it, and probably left Article V so brief precisely because they expected it; but also because contract law is, after all, just a refined set of logical principles to determine whether parties have agreed to bind themselves. Authorities on constitutional amendments have frequently applied principles of contract law to the amending process: see, e.g., Jameson, *Constitutional Conventions* 629-33 (4th ed. 1887); Orfield, *Amending the Federal Constitution* 52 (1942).

It should also be remembered that the amending process was seen as an important bulwark against possible abuses of Federal power: "We may safely rely on the disposition of the State legislatures to erect barriers against encroachments of the national authority." *(The Federalist* No. 85, Hamilton). Thus, while Congress can reasonably be regarded as having implied power to prescribe rules of procedure in the amending process, such rules must necessarily be of the "housekeeping" variety, and cannot be used as a pretext for enlarging the substantive power of Congress as against the states. Congress cannot, for instance, apply a standard for discerning when a state has given its consent which is not genuinely calculated to detect such content. See Note, 85 Harv. L. Rev. 1612, 1617-18 (1972); Comment, 37 La. L. Rev. 896, 904 (1977).

Finally, experience has strengthened the view that the amending process should be used only infrequently, on issues on which a broad consensus exists. This suggests a canon of construction --- whether to comport with the intent of the Framers, or as a prudential means of protecting the Constitution from hasty alteration which might not reflect an enduring consensus --- under which ambiguities in Article V should be resolved in favor of the interpretation which would make amendment more difficult. See authorities cited in Comment, 37 La. L. Rev. 896, 898-900 (1977). It is important to remember that a rule prescribed with a "nice" amendment in mind will be a precedent for "bad" amendments in the future.

These principles of construction can be summarized by saying that ordinary contract law should almost always fill in any gaps in Article V; but that in any event, no construction is admissible which would artificially enhance the Federal role in the amending

---

Literature distributed by Phyllis Schlafly's organization argued that the Equal Rights Amendment was unconstitutional. This legal memo invoked what it considered the original intent of the founders of the nation—including Alexander Hamilton and James Madison—to oppose the ERA.

Members of the Family Rights Coalition picket the women's convention in Houston, Texas, in November 1977. Its supporters claimed that the "grass roots" of America was opposed to abortion.

battle over separate facilities for blacks and whites, antifeminists warned of "desexegration," where men and women would be forced to share everything, including combat duty in war. The specter of homosexual marriages hovered over anti-ERA pronouncements, as did concern about men and women using the same toilets—maybe even the same showers. Where would it all end, if not in the destruction of everything one cherished about the family?

Anti-abortion forces played a variation on the same themes. According to Connie Marshner, the essence of the "pro-choice" argument was that women should be able to put Me first, ignoring the fact that the creation of a fetus was divinely sanctioned, and therefore elimination of the fetus was both a sin and an act of murder. Although Catholics were most likely to become active in "pro-life" groups, as they were called, many Protestants joined also, usually from conservative churches that valued traditional family life as the cornerstone of a virtuous society. According to the National Right to Life group, people who supported women's right to abort a fetus were attacking motherhood, devaluing the sanctity of life, and possibly preventing some future Einstein or Edison from growing to maturity to help the world. By showing motion pictures (based on ultrasound) of a fetus moving around a woman's womb during the third month of pregnancy, these Right to Life groups powerfully portrayed their antagonists as baby-killers.

Clearly, these were neither simple issues, nor were they without transforming emotional force. One could easily become fanatical about women's rights—on either side of the issue. The "click" that a reader of *Ms.* experienced when she heard a male employer refer to his 45-year-old secretary as a "girl" could readily occur on the other side if a Roman Catholic mother of four children heard a physician who performed abortions talk about routinely disposing of 25 fetuses in one day. At what point did women's rights clash head on with the rights of religious freedom? And who was to decide what policies most effectively served the greater good of the community?

All of this turmoil occurred in the midst of a major conservative revival. Richard Nixon had won the Presidency in 1968 by claiming to speak on behalf of the Silent Majority. Insisting that he would restore law and order, resist permissiveness, and strike out against the excesses of antiwar demonstrators and other protestors, Nixon assumed leadership of a cultural war against the most radical of the 1960s social movements. He promised that as President he would appoint conservative, Southern judges to the Supreme Court; fight busing for purposes of racial integration; and defend traditional family values against feminists and others who demanded more child care centers, abortion reform, and sexual freedom.

The dove on George McGovern's campaign button symbolized his opposition to the war in Vietnam. He also became a symbol of other liberal causes, including women's rights.

The 1972 Presidential campaign became, in essence, a referendum on cultural change. George McGovern, the Democratic Presidential nominee, supported amnesty for Vietnam War protestors who had fled to Canada rather than be drafted. He also favored legalization of marijuana. In addition, the party implemented a quota system of representation at the Democratic convention, with racial minorities and women given a larger share of seats than ever before. Nixon, in turn, portrayed McGovern as the embodiment of the counterculture who spoke on behalf of feminism, student radicals, and environmental extremists. As Nixon defined it, the election was to determine whose values would control America—those associated with the traditional family, patriotism, and respect for authority, or those connected to attacks on the family, encouragement of dissent, and rebellion against middle-class morality. Although gender equality was just one of the issues pivotal to the choice that American voters would make, it was also an issue that affected almost every American: It literally entered the most private spaces where people lived as well as public policy debates.

Dianne Chavis was one of those people initially perplexed by the issue. Born in South Carolina in 1953, she had grown up with fairly conventional beliefs. She was not well off, but neither was she poor. After graduating from high school in 1968, she went to a local community college for two years to study to become a dental assistant. Through her training there, she met her husband, who was completing his specialty training in orthodontics. The two moved to the suburb of a larger metropolitan area and within five years had two children. Dianne stayed at home to take care of them. Fully engaged by her activities as a mother and member of the community, Dianne seemed to be the kind of woman *McCall's* would portray as the ideal young wife.

Then two momentous events took place. The first came when

Dianne's older daughter was almost killed by a delivery truck backing out of a driveway. For more than two weeks, she hovered between life and death, and when she finally did recover, it was only after months of therapy and care. The second event was in many ways a direct response to the first. Dianne experienced a religious conversion. She had been a routine churchgoer in her youth, and she and her husband occasionally attended the local Methodist church. But when her daughter was injured, Dianne met another woman at the hospital who was a devoted member of a Baptist evangelical church in the area. That woman seemed so enveloped by her faith that it informed and inspired every part of her life. It strengthened not only her but those she came into contact with. And Dianne was one of these. Through long hours of intense and intimate conversation, Dianne became convinced that she too should turn her life over to Jesus. The next month she was baptized at the evangelical church and started to go to weekly Bible study classes as well as Sunday school and church services. She was a "born-again" Christian.

Dianne's new-found faith not only strengthened her in her daily struggle to help her daughter recover. It also gave her a new perspective on some of the issues that she and the other women in her neighborhood talked about in their backyards. Dianne became convinced by her minister that the family was imperiled by the changes taking place in society and that the deepest threat came from those who were trying to unsettle and subvert the roles that husbands and

Fundamentalist Christian churches, particularly in the South, advocated literal interpretation of the Bible and traditional roles for women and men. Their conservative philosophy was completely at odds with the feminist movement.

wives played. According to the Bible, Dianne said, God had placed men in charge of the household. They were to act on behalf of the well-being of the family, according to God's wishes. Women, in turn, were to be subject to men, offering support and love in their roles as wives and mothers. Both husband and wife—and their children— were to mirror the dictates of God as reflected in the teachings of the Bible.

Consistent with her new beliefs, Dianne became a subscriber to the Moral Majority newsletter. In keeping with the political agenda put forward by conservative politicians, the Moral Majority set out to fight the evils of secular humanism, including those associated with feminism, the ERA, and the campaign for reproductive freedom. Dianne became convinced through studying her newsletter and talking with her friends at church that the ERA would totally destroy all that gave coherence and meaning to her life. It would fragment and corrupt the discipline and authority that God had ordained for the family. And by sanctioning homosexual relationships, it would undo the only means by which God had provided for the perpetuation of his kingdom—the monogamous, heterosexual family.

Dianne was not a rabblerouser. But she knew what she had come to believe and that she must act on that belief. Hence, she joined the organization committed to defeating the ratification of the ERA in her state, agreed to help send out mailings for the Right to Life group in her community, and took as her personal charge the responsibil-

'Supreme Court, indeed! Get back in your place, woman!'

This 1981 cartoon pits Sandra Day O'Connor, the first woman justice of the U.S. Supreme Court, against Jerry Falwell, leader of the Moral Majority. O'Connor voted to uphold the Court's ruling in Roe v. Wade.

The signs carried by these anti-ERA demonstrators on Wall Street reflect the fears of women who considered the amendment a threat to traditional "family values."

ity to bear witness to her faith in her neighborhood conversations with the other women on her block. Many of them had little sympathy with the Moral Majority, and some believed strongly in the ERA and in a woman's right to control her own body. But they understood at least some of the things that Dianne had been through. And thereafter they knew that they would have to consider the depth and conviction of her beliefs on these issues before they could take sides.

Judy Morgan was seven years older than Dianne. She had grown up in a poor household, then had worked her way through college and gotten married immediately after graduation to her college sweetheart, Ted. He was an ambitious account executive who quickly rose through the corporate ranks to become one of the leading officials of his company. He traveled a great deal, frequently taking Judy with him. They had two boys born at the end of the 1960s. The family lived in a New York suburb, not too distant from Ted's office. Judy worked part-time at the local school but spent most of her time in the home, raising the children, helping Ted with his career through entertaining and socializing with other wives, and enjoying their comfortable life-style.

Judy thought of herself as an educated, independent woman. She was active in the local PTA, read magazines like *Harper's* and *The Atlantic,* and ordinarily voted for the Democratic party. She followed closely the emergence of the women's liberation movement, and like most Americans of her class and age group, spent more than a few evenings talking about the new feminism. But Judy was bothered by many of the ideas she associated with the women's movement. It was not that she did not believe women should have equal rights with men or that they should not enjoy equal access to careers and job opportunities. But she resented deeply the implication she heard in much feminist literature that anyone who did not have a career competing with men was a failure and that women who stayed in the home and fulfilled more conventional roles were without value in the society.

Too often, she thought, feminists were not only judging men for being sexist but were also judging women for being behind the times if they did not get on the feminist bandwagon and renounce their prior activities. It was as if a woman who liked to cook, enjoyed raising children, and took pleasure in making a fine home should feel as though she had betrayed her sex. The aura of condescension and snobbishness that seemed to characterize some feminist pronouncements on women's traditional roles was offensive and irritating. If women's rights activists wanted to have a career and challenge men, by all means let them do it. But let them also respect women who made other choices, even if those choices turned out to be traditional in nature.

For Judy, then, the issue was not whether to be a feminist or an antifeminist, but rather to have the freedom to be herself. She did not want to be told she either had to be for complete freedom of lifestyle or totally in the other camp. She believed in the rights of consenting adults to practice whatever kind of sex they wished, but she resented those who declared that a gay or lesbian life-style was more conducive to freedom and fulfillment than a heterosexual marriage. She thought that under certain circumstances women should have the right to abort an unwanted pregnancy. But she also believed that certain limits on that freedom were permissible, including waiting periods, counseling, and a restricted time frame within which an abortion could take place. Judy thought the ERA was a good idea, but she did not approve of women going into combat or living in trenches alongside men. In short, she occupied a middle-of-the-road position on most issues involving feminism, and she was angry that people on both her left and her right were denying her the freedom to occupy that space.

Finally, there was Barbara Harris, an African-American woman who had dropped out of high school to have her first child in the early 1960s. Barbara Harris believed strongly in women's rights as a theoretical goal. After all, she had demonstrated and crusaded for black rights. But most of what she heard from the new women's liberation movement sounded strangely irrelevant to her life. It was all well and good to talk about having a career and shedding sexual stereotypes. But there were not many black women she knew who were in a position to take advantage of those opportunities. The main problem in the black community, as she saw it, was the need for more men to remain committed to building and sustaining traditional nuclear families. She wanted black men to assume and carry out the role of breadwinner, not be free of it.

All the criticism of the nuclear family and traditional sex roles that Harris heard from feminists in the media seemed to reflect a

In 1980, 41 percent of black families were headed by women. Many black women became more concerned with shoring up the erosion in black family life than in working for broader roles for women in the public arena.

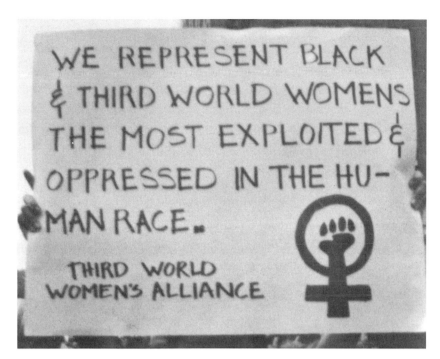

WE REPRESENT BLACK & THIRD WORLD WOMENS THE MOST EXPLOITED & OPPRESSED IN THE HUMAN RACE.

THIRD WORLD WOMEN'S ALLIANCE

Women of color faced discrimination on two fronts: gender and race. Often, they found the need to form organizations separate from "mainstream" white feminist groups.

distinctly white, middle-class perspective. Black women wanted to preserve and strengthen their relationships with black men, not attack those men. Racial solidarity—not division—seemed the most important priority for African Americans, and to the extent that feminism set women against men, it was a threat to be avoided, not a challenge to be welcomed.

Black women supported better pay and greater job opportunities for all women, and they believed in better and more accessible child care facilities. But in too many instances it seemed that white women wanted careers and high-paying jobs so that they could hire black women to take care of their children, without paying them a decent wage. Even the emphasis on reproductive freedom could mean something different in the black community than in the white. Children were valued highly in the African-American culture. What if the focus on abortion was, as some black men said, simply an effort by white people to prevent the black community from growing in size and strength?

Thus, even as the feminist movement appeared to be the dominant force in American society at the beginning of the 1970s, there were counterforces at work mitigating and undercutting the likelihood of a feminist triumph. As it turned out, according to the polls conducted in the early 1980s, 20 percent of the American people were *for* abortion under all circumstances and 20 percent were *against* abortion under all circumstances. But that left 60 percent in the middle, willing to consider a variety of restrictions or controls that might modify *Roe* v. *Wade.* Similarly, although a majority of women and men said they supported the ERA, there was enough energy on the other side to pose a serious challenge to ratification. It required approval by three-fourths of the state legislatures in the country for the ERA to become part of the Constitution. Many of those legislatures that had not yet approved the ERA by the mid-1970s were in those parts of the South where conservative constituencies were strongest.

Moreover, despite the cresting of social protest in the late 1960s, those on the other side were not about to roll over and play dead. As Nixon's campaign had shown, a social and cultural war was being waged, and many Americans who believed that Black Power, the student movement, and women's liberation were gnawing away at the vitals of the nation were ready to fight back. They had powerful resources. The strength of faith in the traditional family, the authority of religion, and the value of patriotism could not be underestimated. Countless Americans shared Dianne Chavis's "born again" beliefs that God had ordained men and women to play profoundly different roles in life. Still others shared the consternation of Judy Morgan at the elitism and judgmental quality of so much feminist rhetoric. It was as if you had violated a feminist ordinance if you had a husband and children and believed in staying home and keeping house. And there were all the poor women—many of them from oppressed racial groups—who had different priorities than white middle-class feminists had. Latina and Asian women, for example, took pride in cultural traditions that gave women a special value as mothers and homemakers. For these women, too, loyalty to family and to racial or ethnic solidarity could easily take precedence over a commitment to a feminist agenda.

The future of women's rights thus appeared to hinge primarily on how different groups of citizens and policymakers in the society responded to the different feminist messages that were being pronounced. Notwithstanding the commitment of many feminists to the ideal of sisterhood across class and race lines, it seemed that women had as many different responses to issues of sex equality as

For Hispanic women, commitment to their culture and traditions was often more important than pursuing feminist goals. Here, dancers participate in a ceremony to celebrate the anniversary of the appearance of the Virgin of Guadalupe near Mexico City in 1531.

men. In the end, how those differences were manifested would determine the success of feminism in bringing transformation and fulfillment to women as a whole.

At the same time it was also clear that a substantial body of Americans, male and female, were prepared to support political figures like Richard Nixon, Jerry Falwell, and Phyllis Schlafly in their effort to return America to conservative social values regarding sex and family life. For these people, feminism—however interpreted— was a hostile force. In the end it seemed that the contest of political wills would have to be resolved by the decisions of those in the middle, not by those who occupied either of the extremes.

CHAPTER 7

THE PERSISTENCE
OF DIFFERENCES

B y the middle of the 1980s there were two generalizations that could be made about women's lives in the United States. The first was that virtually no group in the society had experienced as much change as women had over the preceding three decades. The second was that the changes that had occurred affected women in dramatically different ways, depending on whether they were white or nonwhite, rich or poor, married or divorced. In short, ethnicity, class, and marital status continued to be primary determinants of what happened to women.

Change, of course, was the first thing one noticed when analyzing almost any category of women's behavior over time. In 1957 women bore three to four children in their lifetime. Thirty years later the figure had dropped to less than two. At the height of the Baby Boom that followed World War II, women married, on average, at age 20, had their first child two years later and their last child when they were in their mid-30s. By 1990 the average marriage age had risen to 25—and many women did not marry until their 30s and then had only one child. In the 1950s less than 50 percent of women were sexually active before marriage; by the 1990s the figure had climbed to 80 percent.

Nowhere was the pattern of change more visible than in women's

With the slogan "Raises Not Roses," office workers observe National Secretaries' Day. Such clerical positions remained largely the province of women despite the considerable progress made by the women's movement in ensuring wider opportunities.

employment. In 1960 approximately 30 percent of women worked; three decades later the figure was 60 percent. When John Kennedy was inaugurated in 1961, only one out of four married women held jobs. In 1990 the majority did so. It used to be that mothers of small children rarely entered the labor force. By 1992 more than 60 percent of mothers of children under age six were employed, including 50 percent of those with infants under one. Women not only constituted half the entering classes of law schools and medical schools; they were also expected to make up half the total labor force in the country by the year 2000. Already in the early 1990s they constituted half the bus drivers in America.

Yet the statistics obscured as much as they illuminated. First of all, they hid the degree to which gender itself remained a primary source of inequality. In the mid-1980s, for example, a woman lawyer earned, on average, $33,000, a male lawyer, $53,000. Across the board, women professionals' salaries were only 73 percent of what men professionals took home. In 1984 only 4 percent of working women had incomes higher than $28,000 a year. The figure for men was 26 percent. Women in sales received only half of what men in sales earned. Waitresses took home only 72 percent of what waiters were paid. Overall, men continued to hold 75 percent of the higher paying jobs in the nation. And despite some small progress, women's wages had progressed from 59 percent of what men re-

Gail Winslow, a stockbroker for Ferris & Co. in Washington, D.C., was one of the first women to have visible success in the predominantly male profession.

ceived in 1960 to 70 percent of what men earned in 1990. If cash rewards represented the fundamental barometer of status in America, women were almost as distant from equality with men in 1990 as they had been 30 years before—no matter how many more were in the workplace.

Part of the problem was the degree to which work continued to be allocated, designed, and valued differently according to whether women or men performed it. Going far back into the history of wage labor, there had developed a series of shorthand descriptions to differentiate one kind of work compensation from another. Hence, people talked about a "living wage," a "family wage," and then—quite distinct from the other two—a "woman's wage." The first defined

Nursing, along with teaching and secretarial work, was one of the jobs deemed acceptable for women through most of the 20th century. Until fairly recently, nurses' salaries did not acknowledge the high level of scientific training the job demanded.

A medical secretary in Texas answers the phone for a male doctor. Such a division of labor was typical in the health-care area until fairly recently.

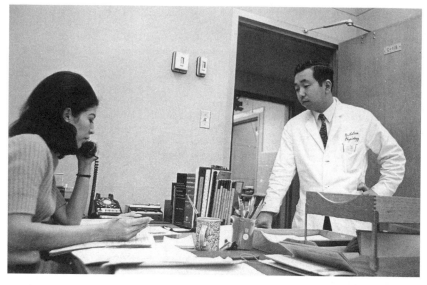

As in medicine, careers in dentistry have also been segregated according to sex. Women were typically employed as dental technicians because of presumed manual dexterity.

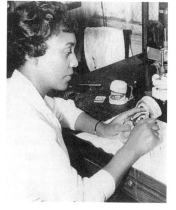

what it was society thought to be necessary for a person to live in dignity, modest comfort, and self-respect. The second described what a *man* should be able to earn in order to provide adequate support for his entire family. Because it was expected that under normal circumstances a husband would work outside the home while his wife reared the children and tended the household, a "family wage" needed to be adequate to sustain four or more people. By contrast, a "woman's wage" was seen as secondary, something extra that women might earn as "pin money," a popular phrase meaning a little "extra" for purchasing frivolous goods. Even though in reality women toiled, just as men did, to support themselves and their families, they were not treated as if that was what they were doing. Rather, there developed the pervasive sense that women's work was inherently worth less than men's.

Notwithstanding all the changes that had taken place in the labor force and in women's employment aspirations, the traditional definition of "women's work" and a "woman's wage" had never changed. It was reflected in two ways: first, the degree to which women doing the same work as men nevertheless received only half the rate of pay; and second, the extent to which women were segregated in certain kinds of jobs that were conceived of by employers, by men, and by the entire society as peculiarly "women's work." Many believed that women's delicate fingers and attention to detail made them particularly qualified to do sewing and other chores requiring dexterity. These skills quickly became generalized to such industries as textiles and garment making. The capacity for monotonous and repetitive labor—the jobs of operatives in canneries or of cigarette rollers in tobacco factories—also became identified as "women's work." In each case, the work women did was viewed as something uniquely theirs to perform and was rewarded not with a "living wage" or a "family wage" but with a "woman's wage."

The result was that the jobs women took in the 30 years after 1960 most often became defined as "women's work," with commensurately lower wages and fewer opportunities for promotion and advancement. Notwithstanding the fact that the proportion of women in the labor force had doubled or that women were now working at almost the same rate of participation as men, they remained overwhelmingly concentrated in "women's jobs," where virtually no men were employed. Thus, 80 percent of women workers were concentrated in just 5 percent of all jobs. Moreover, these 5 percent happened to be the lowest-paying occupations. More than 40 percent of all working women held clerical and sales positions; another 17 per-

The monotony of the file room and the miniskirt of the clerk typify a stereotype that persisted in the 1970s.

The routine work of data entry was often the province of women in large offices.

The situation of bank tellers was of particular concern to women's organizations such as 9 to 5. Very few women were promoted from teller positions, whereas men almost always used the job as a stepping-stone to management.

cent had service jobs. Women dominated the garment industry, they provided virtually all day-care workers, and they monopolized data-entry positions and bank teller jobs. But few of these offered prospects for social or economic upward mobility.

Most of the new jobs created in America after 1970 that were being taken by women were in the service sector. All too often, these jobs paid wages close to the minimum allowed by federal law—barely enough to feed oneself, let alone anyone else. Indeed, statistics from the late 1980s show that 25 percent of all *working* women who were heads of households with children were actually earning incomes that placed them below the poverty level. In far too many cases, then, taking a job defined as "women's work" at a "woman's wage" became a pathway to poverty rather than an open door to self-fulfillment and dignity.

If statistics indicating massive change obscured evidence of persistent gender inequality, they also failed to address other differences *between* women. Certainly a feminist could argue that women's increased employment as well as greater sexual liberation represented positive developments. Part of the "positive" effect was to enable more women to leave unhappy marriages. The divorce rate constituted one of those barometers involving gender that showed the most remarkable rate of change. Before World War II only one in six marriages ended in divorce. Half a century later, one in two marriages was dissolved. Moreover, a correlation existed between female employment and divorce (though that did not mean that women's taking jobs caused divorce). Theoretically, the opportunity to get out of an unhappy marriage and become independent represented part of the progress that accompanied social change and the advancement of women's rights.

Yet in reality divorce often led to the further victimization of women. As part of liberal feminism's assault on sexual distinctions under the law, groups like NOW had supported reform in divorce proceedings that allowed for "no-fault" divorce settlements. These abandoned such traditional practices as having a husband pay "alimony" to his former wife and placed a premium on each person being treated as equal in rights and obligations without regard to gender. When it came right down to it, however, women who had sacrificed their own lives to serve their husbands and families and who had given up careers in order to follow a spouse frequently ended up empty-handed. Laws prescribing community-property settlements (giving each partner half the total family assets) might sound fine. But what did that mean for a woman thrown into the work world without up-to-date job skills, while her former husband was ready to hit the peak of his earning power? Moreover, he might well do so in a state hundreds of miles away, leaving his wife to raise the children except for a few weekends a year. The question did not even begin to confront the fact that only a minority of men paid the child support costs they were assigned as part of the divorce settlement.

Far from being a badge of liberation, then, divorce often became a membership card whose chief benefits were poverty and despair. One scholar who examined the fate of divorced couples in California during the 1970s discovered that in the first year after the divorce the husband's income rose 43 percent, while the wife's standard of living fell by more than 70 percent. As Betty Friedan ruefully noted, "women who had been housewives, who hadn't worked in years, or who made very little money, [now] found themselves divorced with no provision whatsoever for their maintenance or for training for a job to earn real money, and often with the whole responsibility for the children to boot."

One of the other consequences was that poverty became to an ever increasing extent an experience in which women and children were the primary participants. By the 1990s one out of every four

Particularly among immigrant groups, poverty was an increasing threat to the health and education of children. Cutbacks in federal funding for social welfare programs under the Nixon, Reagan, and Bush administrations were part of the problem.

In the 1980s and early 1990s, increasing numbers of women and children, especially African Americans, lived in poverty.

children in America was poor (it had been one in five in 1980), while women constituted 70 percent of the adults who were poor. It was all too confusing. How could one simultaneously be part of a story of liberation and progress and also a victim of institutions and employment practices that remained profoundly discriminatory?

If anything, the picture was even worse for women (and men) who were members of minority groups. From the beginning of American history, race had served as a primary determinant of status, wealth, power, and prestige. It served as the basis for eradicating native peoples from the land, for enslaving generations of Africans and African Americans, and for assigning immigrant groups, whether they be Chinese or Mexicans or Slavs, the most menial and exploitative jobs. But women fared even worse than men in such ethnic minorities. White masters and overseers systematically took sexual advantage of their female slaves, and later—after emancipation—female house servants. Owners of canneries or sweatshop garment factories paid immigrant women lower wages than men, all the while forcing them to work in disease-producing conditions.

Some progress occurred as a result of the labor movement and the civil rights struggle. In the two decades after the 1964 Civil Rights Act was passed, for example, the number of African-American women employed in clerical and other white-collar jobs doubled, from approximately 23 percent to 46 percent. Fewer minority women clustered in domestic service positions, and more had the chance to work on factory floors or in offices from which they had been excluded prior to World War II. Yet black women still remained at the bottom of the economic ladder, earning 60 cents for every dollar earned by the average man as opposed to the 70 cents earned by white women.

The impact of race and ethnicity was clearest of all when it came to the feminization of poverty. Throughout the period of the 1960s, 1970s, and 1980s, the number of female-headed households skyrocketed among all ethnic groups. Still, the figures for black and Latina women were startling. While the number of female-headed households among whites grew from 8 percent to 18 percent, the figure for black women shot up to more than 60 percent, and that for Latina women climbed to 40 percent. These were the same years when poverty resumed its upward climb among ethnic minorities, even as it fell overall among whites. Thus by 1990 approximately 35 percent of black families lived in poverty, as well as 30 percent of Hispanic families. The connection between poverty and being a woman, with children, in charge of a household was dramatic. A child born into a family with both parents present had a 1 in 20 chance of being poor; if there was a father present but not a mother, the chances were 1 in 10; and if the single parent was a woman, the chances soared to 1 in 3.

Behind all the stories about a revolution in women's status, therefore, there existed a complicated, tortured, and often contradictory reality: issues of race and class—interacting with gender—pushed women not upward to a higher level of fulfillment but downward to greater misery and hopelessness. Thus even as some women benefited enormously from the gains that had been won by feminists, countless others saw no change at all in their lives. Indeed, if anything, their situation worsened rather than improved; the promises of women's liberation seemed like a slap in the face given the daily struggle to keep food on the table and hold onto a job paying five dollars an hour at the local Burger King.

In all of this, class and education seemed to be the most important variables. A young college-educated woman from an economically secure background had a world open to her that was strikingly

In the 1980s, many more women entered law and business in professional capacities. Yet it was still not unusual to see a lone woman at a business meeting.

different from that her mother or grandmother had encountered a generation or two earlier. If they worked at all outside the home, it might have been as a secretary, a salesclerk, a nurse, or a teacher. Even then, they were likely to stop work when they married and had a child. The young woman of the 1990s, on the other hand, could go to law school or get a master's degree in business administration. She might then enter a large corporate firm and make a six-figure salary, doing the same kind of work for the same pay as the brightest young man. If she married, it was probable that her husband would be someone with a comparable background. And if they had children, they were likely to hire a nanny to take care of them while they continued to pursue their careers. The sky was the limit, with opportunities and experiences available that would have been unimaginable 30 years earlier.

A young Latina woman born or raised in the South Bronx, on the other hand, faced a very different situation. If she was like half the young people in public school in New York, she would drop out before graduating from high school. There was a good chance she would have a child while still in her teenage years, but would not get married. With no job skills she could find work only at low-paying service establishments. By the time she was 20 she would be locked into a cycle of work and family responsibilities that seemed to offer little opportunity for improvement. Not only was the life of the South Bronx woman no better than her mother's or grandmother's; it might even be worse.

The fast-food industry provides many jobs for unskilled minority workers. Though many such companies have instituted management training programs, the majority of lower-level workers are from minority groups.

There were other possibilities, of course. A white (or black) high school graduate who either worked as a secretary for an insurance agency or as a factory operative at General Motors might well find her life better than that of her mother—for which the feminist movement deserved some credit. Greater attention to sexual harassment in the workplace might discourage unwanted advances from male bosses or coworkers. Legal advances for women's rights contributed to higher wages and the opening of some jobs that previously had been restricted to men. If the woman had an unwanted pregnancy, she now could consider terminating it legally.

On balance, however, one of the major problems with feminist advances was that they operated differentially, their benefits largely limited to those women already in a position to be able to take advantage of the new rights that had been won. Nor did the differential decrease over time. When *Roe* v. *Wade* became the law of the land, for example, poor women as well as rich women had access to an abortion. Then, in 1976, Congress prohibited federal funds from being used to pay for abortions for poor women. Subsequently, a series of additional restrictions was enacted to circumscribe women's right to an abortion, including a 24-hour waiting period and the requirement that teenagers notify their parents and get their permission. Women who were well-off had little difficulty coping with these restrictions. But women from culturally conservative and economically disadvantaged backgrounds found the restrictions almost impossible. What had once seemed like a victory of feminism that af-

In 1976 Harvard Law School celebrated 25 years of women graduates. The keynote speaker was Professor Ruth Bader Ginsberg of Columbia Law School, who attended Harvard from 1956 to 1958 and in 1993 became the second woman appointed to the U.S. Supreme Court.

fected all women soon came in reality to have a distinctly middle- and upper-class tinge to it.

Similarly, government programs designed to force companies and universities to open doors previously closed to women had little impact on those clustered in sex-segregated, low-paying jobs. Affirmative action occasionally worked well as a means of giving women lawyers access to jobs at law firms that previously hired only white men, or as a means of providing women professors opportunities to be hired in departments that had never considered women scholars before. But affirmative action meant little to women who were data processors working side by side with other women in a giant computer pool (unless it meant that some men were hired), or to operatives at a textile mill who had neither the education nor the training to qualify for a management-level opening. In short, affirmative action—and other equal opportunity programs—tended to benefit those with preexisting credentials that enabled them to move forward, not to open new possibilities to those stuck in sex-segregated and low-paying positions.

On the other hand, programs that might have been of greater value to the mass of women in the workplace either were not imple-

For working women of all socioeconomic groups, finding day care for their children is an overwhelming concern.

mented or were rejected. Working-class and minority women had no need greater than adequate child care for their young children—child care that would not only permit them to hold decent jobs, but would also provide for their children the kind of medical care, nutrition, and educational stimulation that might break the cycle of poverty and improve the children's chances for a better life. Congress enacted such a program in 1972. Called the Comprehensive Child Development Act, it would have created day-care centers throughout the country, with places available to all children regardless of ability to pay. But President Nixon vetoed the measure on the grounds that it would undermine the strength of the nuclear family. Well-off people, of course, could afford to pay for their own child care. But poor women did not have that option, and most were forced to rely on makeshift arrangements.

"Comparable worth" was another idea that, if enacted and upheld by the courts, might have significantly improved the economic status of millions of women workers. Equal pay legislation in the past had focused on securing equal compensation for women who performed the same work as men. Yet such laws failed to address the underlying problem of job segmentation—the fact that most women

Los Angeles Working Women enlisted the aid of actress Jane Fonda to distribute an employment questionnaire.

worked with other women and did not hold the same jobs as men. On the other hand, if the skills required for a job could be measured and compared with skills needed for other jobs, it might be possible to arrive at a reliable standard that would lead to people with comparable skills being paid comparable wages. In San Jose, California, for example, job investigators found that the skills and training needed by a nurse were approximately comparable to those required for a fire-truck mechanic. Yet the nurse, a woman, earned $9,000 less than the mechanic, a man. Clearly, given the number of women in skilled positions, whether nurses, secretaries, or data processors, a wage scale adjusted to compensate for comparable worth might bring substantial improvement in wages.

In some cities, such as Minneapolis and Seattle, where comparable worth policies were implemented, it made a significant difference. Yet many government officials criticized the idea as unworkable and a violation of the free market system, and courts were inconsistent in upholding comparable worth laws. What the opponents ignored, of course, was that the so-called free market system was in fact based on Neanderthal ideas that women should be confined to "women's work" that paid only a "woman's wage."

It seemed clear that poor, working class, and minority women had ample reason to feel that feminism reflected middle-class priori-

Much of the work of feminist organizations dealt with the concerns of urban and suburban women, particularly professionals. Rural women like these Hispanic agricultural workers have often felt ignored by the movement.

ties and values. To be sure, feminist groups from NOW to Redstockings (a radical feminist group) included attention to working-class issues in their literature and did what they could to press for measures that would be as advantageous to the poor as to the rich. Yet in the end feminist victories seemed to be concentrated in areas designed to protect and promote *individual* rights for those in a position to take advantage of them rather than on issues that might bring *collective* advancement for women of all classes and races. Justifiably or unjustifiably, "feminism" became associated in the public eye with well-groomed, highly articulate women in business suits who sat around boardroom tables or frequented centers of power. It did not seem to embody a program that an Irish-Catholic mother of four who worked in a shoe factory could identify with. Nor did it advance a perspective full of empathy toward a black single mother who was a high school dropout. Clearly, there were groups that tried to bridge that chasm, and there certainly were black and Hispanic women who occupied prominent positions in feminist organizations. Nevertheless, it was hard to escape the conclusion that ethnicity and class remained powerful obstacles to universal sisterhood or that the experience of women who were poor and from minority backgrounds in the 30 years after 1960 bore little in common with the experience of those who were middle and upper class and well-educated. No dilemma would be more important to solve if women's story in the 21st century was to be one of both progress and solidarity.

CHAPTER 8

WHERE DO WE GO FROM HERE?

As the nation prepared to greet the year 2000, there were few issues that seemed as critical to the future direction of American society as what happened to women. The changes over the preceding 60 years had been breathtaking. In 1940 the typical woman worker was young, single, and poor. By the mid-1990s she was married and middle-aged, and her job was indispensable for her family to claim middle-class status. On the eve of World War II only one in four women held jobs outside the home. Fifty years later the figure approached three in four. Divorces and remarriage now took place in one of every two unions, as opposed to one in six in 1940. Women medical doctors and lawyers had become almost as familiar a sight as men doctors and lawyers. The nation's First Lady, Hillary Rodham Clinton, was in charge of solving the country's greatest social and economic problem—health care—and women who openly identified themselves as feminists (and some as lesbians) held high government office. The military had decided that women should serve with men in nearly all areas, including some situations of armed combat, and the assumption that women and men should be treated as equals had become a part of the American Creed.

On the other hand, women also remained the primary victims of economic, social, and political inequality in this new society. Even

Susan B. Anthony (a relative of the pioneering woman suffrage advocate) and Bella Abzug were among the "Women on the Move" attending the women's conference in Houston in 1977.

Dianne Rivera-Jean (above), an electrician's mate/fireman leaves a California naval base en route to Somalia, where she will assist in relief efforts of Operation Restore Hope. Lt. Cmdr. Darlene M. Iskra (right), commanding officer of the salvage ship USS Opportune, *was the first woman assigned to command a U.S. Navy ship.*

as 40 percent of the black women in the country took their place alongside white women as full participants in the middle class, and as lawyers, doctors, and business executives, another 40 percent became caught up in an ever-deepening spiral of poverty, unemployment, and social dislocation. If the country as a whole was becoming to an increasing extent a two-tier society, with little in values, resources, or life-style shared in common between the two tiers, women were in the forefront of the division.

To some extent, any social change, good or bad, reveals as much about the larger society as it does about the individuals or groups most involved in the change itself. So it is with the contradictory trends that emerge from considering the fate of American women since the early 1960s. The various feminist movements—so much a part of that process of change—tell us a great deal about what options did and did not exist for those seeking to shape the direction change would take. In addition, the way the society responded to different demands and possibilities may help clarify the direction that future developments will take.

By the mid-1990s policymakers and Americans in general seemed to have struck a compromise on what would be allowed in the way of judicial and constitutional change on women's status. Despite early success in securing support in state legislatures, for example, backers of the Equal Rights Amendment discovered that there was enough opposition to the ERA that there was no chance of persuading three-fourths of the states to ratify it. Constitution. By 1982, time ran out and the battle was to all intents and purposes over. Part of the reason

Much of the opposition to abortion has come from the South, where fundamentalist Christians like these Southern Baptist worshipers have preserved conservative values regarding moral and political issues.

for the defeat was the regional culture in the United States. On virtually any issue involving traditional values, whether it be patriotism, prayer in the schools, or sex roles, the Southern states took a more conservative stance than others. In the end there was enough recalcitrance in the 11 states of the former Confederacy to block the ERA.

Yet that was only part of the story. Those same states now had substantial black populations able to vote after the Voting Rights Act of 1965 went into effect. Black voters helped elect moderate to liberal Democratic senators and representatives, who in turn often voted for progressive programs. Behind the negative votes of state legislatures on the ERA rested a more basic uneasiness with a measure that threatened, from a conservative cultural point of view, to throw out distinctions between women and men that seemed basic to a traditional kind of society. Ultimately, the ERA failed because individuals like Judy Morgan and Dianne Chavis did not wish their legislators to leave traditional values completely behind.

On the other hand, there also seemed to be a consensus that most of the advances made during the height of feminist influence should remain in place. Thus in 1992 in the case of *Webster* v. *Reproductive Health Services,* the Supreme Court finally decided, after years of threatening to overturn *Roe* v. *Wade,* to leave the heart of the decision intact. In keeping with the apparent sentiments of a plurality of the American people, the Court allowed state legislatures to limit women's right to choose an abortion with a whole

A male assistant cares for his boss's five-week-old baby when she is called back from maternity leave for an urgent meeting at the office. The difficulties of finding child care often lead to such impromptu arrangements.

series of restraints. Some of these restraints came dangerously close to eliminating the right to choose entirely. But when called upon to reverse the abortion decision itself, the Court pulled back.

In each of these instances there appeared to be a natural tendency to round off the rough edges of more extreme positions taken by both pro- and anti-feminists. There had developed more of a give and take process—in some observers' view the only way to temper the antagonism that often accompanied moralistic politics. As Eleanor Holmes Norton, an activist for civil rights and black women's rights, noted, "[Women] must not allow any issue, however important, to displace all others. Otherwise, you and others who must take leadership . . . will risk resentment and backlash from within the women's movement and from our allies who consistently lend their support to our issues."

The larger question was whether feminists and others could develop a program that reflected not only existing feminist concerns for advancing the rights of individual women, but also the concerns of other groups for a more just and fair society. In many European societies it had long been traditional for women reformers to incorporate their objectives for women into larger social democratic policies that included women but were not limited exclusively to women's rights. Thus, for example, Sweden and Finland enacted laws that made parental leave, with pay, available to every family with a new baby. In most cases used by mothers rather than fathers, such parental-leave laws made staying home and taking care of a child a basic human and social right. At the same time, it ensured that whichever parent stayed home, he or she would lose neither their job nor their seniority. Similarly, many European states provided government-run child-care facilities as a basic educational and social right to every newborn. Again, women might be the chief beneficiaries, but the rationale was what was best for the entire society. The overall approach was to emphasize what joined people together as part of a common society, not what divided them.

There was at least a chance that American society might seek to move in a similar direction. Focusing attention on national health care as a social priority, for example, meant dealing directly with the needs of poor women and children, who would presumably derive the greatest benefit from such health care; yet the program would not advertise itself as a feminist program but rather as one that any society committed to the mutual well-being of its members should pursue. Similarly, new commitments to child care, parental leave, and enforcement of child support arrangements could be presented as pro-family, pro-community measures designed to serve the well being of everyone, even though women—and especially poor women— might well gain the most.

No issues have been a greater source of injustice and inequality in American society than those shaped by gender, race, and class. Through the extraordinary sacrifice of countless activists, American society had been persuaded to address barriers of race and gender that persisted in American law. In the 50 years after World War II, enormous progress was made in freeing individual Americans from the straitjackets that denied them equal opportunity because they were born black or Puerto Rican or female. That record of achievement made the second half of the 20th century truly a time of liberation.

But there remained the fact that a new freer America was still a two-tier America, where class, combined with race and gender, still functioned to leave millions of people unable to take advantage of any of the rights newly won by civil rights advocates and feminists. If Americans could move with as much energy and purpose in the new century to extend basic human rights and decent living conditions to those left on the second tier, then perhaps the long struggle to secure true equality between women and men, white and non-white could finally be won.

Escorted by all six women members of the U.S. Senate— Carol Moseley-Braun, Barbara Boxer, Nancy Landon Kassebaum, Patty Murray, Barbara Mikulski, and Dianne Feinstein—Hillary Rodham Clinton prepares to talk with the Senate about President Clinton's proposed health care reforms.

CHRONOLOGY

1963	Report of the President's Commission on the Status of Women; *The Feminine Mystique* by Betty Friedan; Congress passes Equal Pay Act
1964	Enactment of the Civil Rights Act, including Title VII barring discrimination in hiring on the basis of sex
1965	"Sex and Caste: A Kind of Memo" by Casey Hayden and Mary King circulates among members of Student Non-Violent Coordinating Committee (SNCC)
1966	National Organization for Women (NOW) formed by Betty Friedan and others to protest the failure of the Equal Employment Opportunity Commission (EEOC) to enforce civil rights for women
1967–68	First stirrings of women's liberation movement
1968	Protest at Miss America contest in Atlantic City
1970	Strike and march by women activists to commemorate the 50th anniversary of the ratification of woman suffrage
1972	*Ms.* magazine begins publication; Shirley Chisholm campaigns for Democratic nomination for President; Congress passes Equal Rights Amendment (ERA,) and it is submitted to the states for ratification; Phyllis Schlafly forms National Committee to Stop ERA; President Richard Nixon vetoes Comprehensive Child Development Act
1973	Supreme Court decides, in *Roe* v. *Wade*, in favor of a woman's right to have an abortion
1974	Nine to Five, an organization of women clerical workers, formed; Coalition of Labor Union Women formed
1976	Congress passes Hyde Amendment, prohibiting the use of federal funds for abortions for poor women
1982	Time expires for ratification of the ERA, and the amendment is defeated
1990	First veto by President George Bush of the Parental Leave bill
1992	Second veto by President George Bush of the Parental Leave bill; Supreme Court, in *Webster* v. *Reproductive Health Services*, upholds *Roe* v. *Wade*
1993	Enactment of Parental Leave Act; President Bill Clinton appoints Hillary Rodham Clinton to coordinate health care policy

FURTHER READING

A Note on Sources

In the interest of readability, the volumes in this series include no discussion of historiography and no footnotes. As works of synthesis and overview, however, they are greatly indebted to the research and writing of other historians. The principal works drawn on in this volume are among the books listed below.

Women in the 20th Century

Chafe, William H. *The Paradox of Change: American Women in the Twentieth Century.* New York: Oxford University Press, 1991.

Ehrenreich, Barbara. *The Hearts of Men: American Dreams and the Flight from Commitment.* Garden City, N.Y.: Anchor, 1983.

Evans, Sara. *Born for Liberty: A History of Women in America.* New York: Free Press, 1989.

Filene, Peter. *Him/Her/Self: Sex Roles in Modern America.* 2nd ed. Baltimore: Johns Hopkins University Press, 1986.

Linden-Ward, Blanche, and Carol Hurd Green. *Changing the Future: American Women in the 1960s.* New York: Twayne, 1992.

May, Elaine Tyler. *Homeward Bound: American Families in the Cold War Era.* New York: Basic Books, 1988.

Rosenberg, Rosalind. *Divided Lives: American Women in the Twentieth Century.* New York: Hill & Wang, 1992.

Rubin, Lillian. *Worlds of Pain: Life in the Working-Class Family.* New York: Basic Books, 1976.

Wandersee, Winifred. *On the Move: American Women in the 1970s.* New York: Twayne, 1988.

Feminism

Boston Women's Health Book Collective Staff. *Our Bodies, Ourselves.* Rev. 2nd ed. New York: Simon & Schuster, 1976.

Bunch, Charlotte. *Passionate Politics: Feminist Theory in Action.* New York: St. Martin's, 1987.

Cott, Nancy F. *The Grounding of Modern Feminism.* New Haven: Yale University Press, 1987.

Daly, Mary. *Beyond God the Father.* Boston: Beacon Press, 1973.

Davis, Angela. *Woman, Race and Class.* New York: Random House, 1981.

Echols, Alice. *Daring to Be Bad: Radical Feminism in America, 1967–1975.* Minneapolis: University of Minnesota Press, 1989.

Eisenstein, Zillah. *The Radical Future of Liberal Feminism.* White Plains, N.Y.: Longman, 1981.

Firestone, Shulamith. *The Dialectic of Sex: The Case for Feminist Revolution.* New York: Morrow, 1970.

Friedan, Betty. *The Feminine Mystique.* New York: Norton, 1963.

Friedan, Betty. *It Changed My Life*. New York: Random House, 1976.

Friedan, Betty. *The Second Stage*. New York: Summit, 1981.

Greer, Germaine. *The Female Eunuch*. New York: McGraw-Hill, 1971.

hooks, bell. *Ain't I a Woman: Black Women and Feminism*. Boston: South End Press, 1991.

hooks, bell. *Talking Back: Thinking Feminism, Thinking Black*. Boston: South End Press, 1989.

Hull, Gloria, et al. *All the Women Are White, All the Blacks Are Men, But Some of Us Are Brave*. New York: Feminist Press, 1982.

Millett, Kate. *Sexual Politics*. Garden City, N.Y.: Doubleday, 1970.

Morgan, Robin, ed. *Sisterhood is Powerful*. New York: Random House, 1970.

Reuther, Rosemary Radford. *Sexism and God Talk: Toward a Feminist Theology*. Boston: Beacon Press, 1983.

The Equal Rights Amendment

Berry, Mary Frances. *Why the ERA Failed: Politics, Women's Rights and the Amending Process*. Bloomington: Indiana University Press, 1986.

Hoff-Wilson, Joan, ed. *Rights of Passage: The Past and Future of the ERA*. Bloomington: Indiana University Press, 1986.

Mansbridge, Jane. *Why We Lost the ERA*. Chicago: University of Chicago Press, 1986.

Mathews, Donald, and Jane Sherron DeHart. *Gender and Politics: Cultural Fundamentalism and the ERA*. New York: Oxford University Press, 1990.

Women's Liberation Movement

Evans, Sara. *Personal Politics: The Origins of Women's Liberation in the Civil Rights Movement*. New York: Knopf, 1979.

Freeman, Jo. *The Politics of Women's Liberation*. New York: David McKay, 1975.

Harrison, Cynthia. *On Account of Sex: The Politics of Women's Issues, 1945–1968*. Berkeley: University of California Press, 1988.

Hartmann, Susan M. *From Margin to Mainstream: American Women and Politics Since 1960*. New York: Knopf, 1989.

Hole, Judith, and Ellen Levine, *Rebirth of Feminism*. New York: Quadrangle, 1971.

Rupp, Leila, and Verta Taylor. *Survival in the Doldrums: The American Women's Rights Movement, 1945–60*. New York: Oxford University Press, 1987.

Women on the Right

Crawford, Alan. *Thunder on the Right*. New York: Pantheon, 1980.

Klatch, Rebecca. *Women of the New Right*. Philadelphia: Temple University Press, 1987.

Schlafly, Phyllis. *The Power of the Positive Woman*. New Rochelle, N.Y.: Arlington House, 1977.

Abortion

Ginsburg, Faye. *Contested Lives: The Abortion Debate in an American Community*. Berkeley: University of California Press, 1989.

Luker, Kristin. *Abortion and the Politics of Motherhood.* Berkeley: University of California Press, 1984.

Petchesky, Rosalind. *Abortion and Woman's Choice: The State, Sexuality and Reproductive Freedom.* New York: Longman, 1984.

Women in the Civil Rights Movement

Crawford, Vicki, Jacqueline Anne Rouse, and Barbara Woods, eds. *Women in the Civil Rights Movement: Trailblazers and Torchbearers, 1941–1965.* New York: Carlson, 1990.

King, Mary. *Freedom Song: A Personal Story of the 1960s.* New York: Morrow, 1987.

Moody, Anne. *Coming of Age in Mississippi.* New York: Dial Press, 1968.

Murray, Pauli. *The Autobiography of a Black Artist, Feminist, Lawyer, Priest, and Poet.* Originally published as *Song in a Weary Throat.* Knoxville: University of Tennessee Press, 1989.

Robinson, Jo Ann. *The Montgomery Bus Boycott and the Women Who Started It.* Edited by David J. Garrow. Knoxville: University of Tennessee Press, 1987.

Rothschild, Mary Aikin. *A Case of Black and White: Northern Volunteers and the Southern Freedom Summers.* Westport, Conn.: Greenwood, 1982.

Marriage, Family, and Children

Evans, Sara, and Barbara Nelson, *Wage Justice: Comparable Worth and the Paradox of Technocratic Reform.* Chicago: University of Chicago Press, 1989.

Faludi, Susan. *Backlash.* New York: Crown, 1991.

Hewlett, Sylvia. *When the Bough Breaks: The Cost of Neglecting Our Children.* New York: Basic Books, 1991.

Hochschild, Arlie. *Second Shift: Working Parents and the Revolution at Home.* New York: Viking, 1989.

Jones, Jacqueline. *Labor of Love, Labor of Sorrow: Black Women, Work, and the Family from Slavery to the Present.* New York: Basic Books, 1985.

Weitzman, Lenore. *The Divorce Revolution: The Unexpected Social and Economic Consequences for Women and Children in America.* New York: Free Press, 1985.

Autobiographics and Biographies

Blau, Justine. *Betty Friedan.* New York: Chelsea House, 1990.

Daffron, Carolyn. *Gloria Steinem.* New York: Chelsea House, 1988.

Henry, Sondra, and Emily Taitz. *Betty Friedan: Fighter for Women's Rights.* Hillside, N.J.: Enslow, 1990.

Hoff, Mark. *Gloria Steinem: The Women's Movement.* Boston: Houghton Mifflin, 1992.

Patrick, Diane. *Coretta Scott King.* New York: Franklin Watts, 1991.

Scheader, Catherine. *Shirley Chisholm: Teacher and Congresswoman.* Hillside, N.J.: Enslow, 1990.

Steinem, Gloria. *Outrageous Acts and Everyday Rebellions.* New York: NAL/Dutton, 1986.

INDEX

Picture Credits

Michael Alexander, 1979: 95; Archives of Industrial Society, Hillman Library, University of Pittsburgh: 21, 66, 68, 118-B; © 1964 George Ballis: 19; Ball State University, A.M. Bracken Library, Archives and Special Collections: 33; Courtesy the Bancroft Library, University of California, Berkeley: 15, 59-T, 92; Bentley Historical Library, University of Michigan: 46, 57; City of New York, Human Resources Administration/Gregory Bell: 122; Department of Defense, Still Media Records Center, Washington, D.C.: 132-L, 132-R; Photo courtesy Girl Scouts of the U.S.A.: 37; Courtesy Harvard Law School, photo by Brad Herzog: 125-B; Courtesy of International Business Machines Corporation: 124; John F. Kennedy Library: 10, 29; © Bettye Lane: 64, 69, 94, 108; LBJ Library Collection/O.J. Rapp: 42; Library of Congress: 60, 67, 74, 81, 90, 93, 116; From the collection of David Loehr: 14; Courtesy Maytag: 23; The George Meany Memorial Archives: 121 (negative # 486); Photo courtesy Miss America Organization: 49-L; National Archives: 34, 36, 40, 44, 72, 104, 117, 128, 130; 9 to 5, National Association of Working Women: 114, 120, 127; Oberlin College Archives: 48, 63; Courtesy *off our backs,* photo by Nina: 80; © Oliphant 1981, Universal Press Syndicate. Reprinted with permission. All rights reserved: 107; Reuters/Bettmann: 125-T, 135; Franklin Delano Roosevelt Library: 12; © Miriam Schapiro, *Celebrating Women's Lives,* 1986. Acrylic and paper on canvas. Collection: Brevard Art Center and Museum, Melbourne, Florida. Courtesy Steinbaum Krauss Gallery, New York: cover, half-title page (detail); Schlesinger Library, Radcliffe College: 25, 28, 38, 39, 52; Schomburg Center for Research in Black Culture, New York Public Library, Astor, Lenox and Tilden Foundations: 16, 17, 18, 50, 53, 111; Smithsonian Institution: 59-B, 92, 105; Sophia Smith Collection, Smith College, Northampton, Mass.: 62, 70, 75, 83, 84, 86, 88, 101, 103; Southern Baptist Historical Library and Archives, Nashville, Tennessee: 106, 133; *The Tennessean,* Nashville: 54; Ira Toff: 126; Nancy Toff: 134; Photo courtesy of Tupperware: 32; University of Minnesota Archives: 55; University of Missouri-Kansas City, University Archives: 89; University of Texas, the Institute of Texan Cultures, San Antonio, Texas: 20, 113 (*The San Antonio Light* Collection), 118-T, 119 (Zintgraff Collection); UPI/Bettmann: 71, 98, 110; UPI/Bettmann Newsphotos: 49-R, 58; © Washington Post, reprinted by permission of the Washington, D.C., Public Library: 7, 8, 26, 30, 56, 78, 79, 82, 97, 102; Wayne State University, Archives of Labor and Urban Affairs: 24, 43, 91.

William H. Chafe is Alice Mary Baldwin Distinguished Professor of History and chair of the history department at Duke University. He has also served as director of the Duke–University of North Carolina Women's Studies Research Center. Professor Chafe is the author of *The American Woman: Her Changing Social, Political and Economic Roles 1920–1970; Women and Equality: Changing Patterns in American Culture; Civilities and Civil Rights: Greensboro, North Carolina and the Black Struggle for Freedom; The Unfinished Journey: America Since World War II; The Paradox of Change: American Women in the Twentieth Century;* and *Never Stop Running: Allard Lowenstein and the Struggle to Save American Liberalism.* He is coeditor, with Harvard Sitkoff, of *A History of Our Time: Readings in Postwar America,* and general series editor, with Anne Firor Scott, of University Publications of America's women's studies series.

Nancy F. Cott is Stanley Woodward Professor of history and American studies at Yale University. She is the author of *The Bonds of Womanhood: "Woman's Sphere" in New England 1780–1835; The Grounding of Modern Feminism;* and *A Woman Making History: Mary Ritter Beard Through Her Letters,* editor of *Root of Bitterness: Documents of the Social History of American Women,* and co-editor of *A Heritage of Her Own: Towards a New Social History of American Women.*